BEST OF FRIENDS

THE FIRST THIRTY YEARS
OF THE
FRIENDLY STREET POETS

NOTES ON THE EDITORS

Steve Evans is a senior lecturer at Flinders University in the Department of English, Creative Writing and Australian Studies. He has published six books of poetry and edited or written five other books, including four with Kate Deller-Evans.

Kate Deller-Evans has taught academic, professional and creative writing. She has two poetry collections, co-wrote a study skills text, and a self help manual for writers (with Steve Evans), and has edited a number of anthologies.

The couple have long been involved with Friendly Street as readers, listeners, contributors, editors, and committee members. They considered Friendly Street as a wedding venue.

BEST OF FRIENDS

THE FIRST THIRTY YEARS
OF THE
FRIENDLY STREET POETS

Edited by Steve Evans and Kate Deller-Evans

Friendly Street Poets

Wakefield Press

Friendly Street Poets Incorporated
PO Box 43 Rundle Mall
Adelaide
South Australia 5000

in association with

Wakefield Press
1 The Parade West
Kent Town
South Australia 5067

www.friendlystreetpoets.org.au
www.wakefieldpress.com.au

First published 2008

Poet photographs by Gaetano Aiello, taken at the 30th anniversary reading
Venue photographs by Steve Evans

The Friendly Street Committee has attempted to contact every poet
represented in this collection. If your work appears here and you have not
previously been reached regarding this publication, please contact the
committee at the publisher's address.

Back cover artwork by Graham Catt
Cover design by Clinton Ellicott, Wakefield Press
Edited by Steve Evans and Kate Deller-Evans
Typeset by Clinton Ellicott, Wakefield Press
Printed in Australia by Griffin Press, Adelaide

ISBN 978 1 86254 793 3

**Government
of South Australia**

Arts SA

Friendly Street Poets Inc. is supported by
the **South Australian Government**
through Arts SA.

CONTENTS

PREFACE

Friendly Street is not an actual place name. The street does not exist and never has existed ... yet it appears in the *Oxford Literary Guide to Australia* and taxi drivers seem to know where to find it.

Christopher Bantick 1993

If Friendly Street is not on any map but can be reached by taxi, just what is it? Famous poet and academic, the late Vincent Buckley, once described Friendly Street as 'the best poetry reading in Australia'. Editors Jeff Guess and Donna McSkimming called it 'an inspiration, a deadline, a social occasion, an information centre, a form of publishing and a performance art evening'. Perhaps the most succinct description was from Carol Treloar: 'Friendly Street is the pulse of local poetry'.

Friendly Street is a monthly gathering of people with a shared interest in writing, reading and publishing poetry, and it has been running in Adelaide since the end of 1975. These aficionados have maintained Australia's longest running series of community poetry readings and nurtured the careers of many writers who are now rightly regarded as important poets in this country. The significance of their achievement can be gauged by the fact that Friendly Street has held more than 300 readings (roughly 15,000 individual performances) and published over 70 books. It continues to provide a space for poets to perform their work to a live audience, a factor often overlooked for what it may add to a poem's subsequent success on the page.

As Melbourne poet Lynette Kirby said, 'to read a poem in public is to bring it alive in a different way'. All of the poems published in the annual anthologies have been performed at Friendly Street, so their authors have had the chance to deliver them with a more acute sense of the dynamics of the spoken word in mind, to receive audience feedback, and to edit their work accordingly.

This book exists because Friendly Street is a major contributor to Australian poetry, through its readings and its publications. Poet Bev Roberts wrote that 'Adelaide's Friendly Street is . . . distinguished from counterparts in other cities – like Melbourne's La Mama Poetica – by its role as a nurturer and publisher of poetry'. She described its publication record as 'a remarkable achievement on the Australian publishing scene and evidence of the continuing life and strength of poetry in one small state'.

A review of Friendly Street history is also timely given that we are in an era when the reliance on community arts activities is ever more critical. Larger publishers have essentially abandoned poetry under pressure to make each of their lines profitable in the short run: no more cross-subsidies or long-view budgets. Federal funding is tight and less disposed to supporting the arts, it seems. If poets formed themselves into cricket teams they would have a better chance of drawing on some of the government and corporate largesse currently directed into sports – provided there were sufficient votes, advertising revenues or TV rights involved.

In recounting some of the major features of the history of Friendly Street, we are conscious that we come to the task with our own personal connections to it. At different times, both of us have served on the Friendly Street Committee, so we have seen its management processes from behind the counter, so to speak. We are also fortunate to have had poems in the annual anthologies when the editors liked them enough and, when the manuscript assessors gave the nod, we have had collections of poems published by Friendly Street in association with Wakefield Press. The Friendly Street community has been a significant one in our lives as poets and we still count on its existence to provide a group of like-minded people with whom to satisfy that frequent need for a shot of verse.

When the opportunity came to look back over the first 30 years of Friendly Street for this book, we grabbed it – with only a rough idea of the amount of travel, archive research, interviews, and reading of Friendly Street publications that would be involved. It's axiomatic that the job is always bigger than one guesses, and this task has taken up large chunk of our lives. Regardless, Friendly Street deserves to have its history updated and the world needs an anthology that shows off the kind of poetry that has kept Friendly Street at the forefront of poetry publishing in Australia.

The beginnings of Friendly Street have been documented several times. In 1992, Jeri Kroll and Barry Westburg (both Friendly Street regulars of the time) edited *Tuesday Night Live*, a volume of poetry drawn from the first fifteen years of Friendly Street anthologies, plus a history of the organisation that was heralded by critic Jeff Doyle as 'essential reading for anyone interested in recent Australian Poetry'. It is a comfort to your editors to learn how initially hesitant and then protracted was the process of getting *Tuesday Night Live* together. The task then was a large one and, with the constant spectre of funds to publish the work slipping away, the Friendly Street Committee was nervous about how it might eventually be produced, but it did emerge – and to acclaim. The book that you now hold looks back at the whole of the first thirty years and in doing so it offers some fresh material and a new perspective on that earlier period, as well as an account of events since. In fact, we held off re-reading *Tuesday Night Live* until we had completed a solid draft of *Best of Friends*, in order not to complicate one with the other.

We did not scrutinise the financial records. Our concerns were more to do with the nature of the gathering called Friendly Street – its people, its activities, its achievements, and its significance. In fact, the records of money matters available to us were incomplete, and for the period to 1988 were simply unavailable. Coincidentally or not, the end of

3

that earlier period is when the finances of Friendly Street almost turned ruinous – but more of that later.

Our choice of poems for this collection was not based on any formula for proportional representation of any kind; of period, or poet, or anything else. That would have been unfair and, in any case, probably unworkable. Instead, we looked for poems that gave us an immediate positive reaction in order to create a volume that would make for stimulating reading, and show the vitality of Friendly Street as a major site of poetry in Australia. We chose no more than one poem per poet and, with one or two exceptions only, restricted poems to just a page. This was done to maximise the variety of poems and poets. The result is an energetic and very satisfying collection, at the price of excluding some other very engaging work. Someone else would doubtless have taken a different slice of poetry to represent Friendly Street through the years, and we know that we had to omit many wonderful pieces to arrive at this collection. We sincerely hope that if the poetry in this book appeals, you will also go to the earlier anthologies for more reading.

Poems can too easily be overworked: as Geoff Page wrote, 'a poet must learn to be dissatisfied – but not, perhaps, too dissatisfied'. We are pleased to observe that there is liveliness and immediacy in poems in this anthology that is refreshing without being overly raw, and it suggests the feeling of a Friendly Street reading. Of course, it would be foolish of us to claim that this book is a direct substitute for the unfolding of a poem as it is performed in front of you. It is, though, an excellent pointer to the energy and pleasure to be felt in being present at a live Friendly Street reading.

Looking back at the successful history of Friendly Street, we know that many people should be celebrated for their contributions. It is not surprising that when an organisation has lasted more than thirty years, some of those who have been associated with it will have passed on. Sadly, the poetry readings have sometimes been prefaced with news of the loss of a well-known figure. Among those, including several who were members of the management committee at some stage, are: Nitu Banerji, Jenny Boult (later known as Magenta Bliss), John Bray, Robert Clark, Caroline Cleland, Junice Direen, Constance Frazer, Nancy Gordon, Flexmore Hudson, Adèle Kipping, Susan McGowan, Allison Moore, Ray Stuart, and Maureen Vale. One of the most significant figures, John Bray, was the former Chief Justice of South Australia. An accessible character with an incisive wit, John was always ready when advice was needed to help the committee through some tortuous legal maze or other. The only time that a Friendly Street reading has been devoted to a single poet was in the July 1995 reading dedicated to John Bray. Unfortunately, he died days before the special evening of short speeches and readings of his work, including a contribution by founding member, Richard Tipping. His bequest enabled the Satura Prize, awarded since for the best poem in each year's anthology, to commemorate John Bray's writing and his valuable assistance to Friendly Street.

We would like to acknowledge the very helpful staff at Special Collections, Academy Library at the Australian Defences Forces Academy (ADFA) who helped us with access to the papers up to 1988 that Graham Rowlands lodged there. Rowlands has had a long connection with Friendly Street and was a key figure in the early years of its operation. In the initial years, poets whose work appeared in the new Friendly Street Reader celebrated with a reading at its launch, and an edited recording was then put to air on Radio 5UV's *Writers' Radio* program, which Jeri Kroll ran. Like Rowlands, Kroll has been on the Friendly Street management committee. The scripts of her comments from these shows but, unfortunately, not the actual recordings, are also now held at ADFA, and we looked at those too.

We would especially like to thank Gaetano Aiello and the

members of the Friendly Street Committee who entrusted us with much of the post-1988 archives. David Adès, another past convenor of Friendly Street, was especially generous with his time and access to his own records. We were able to research the background stories to Friendly Street activities: the correspondence; minutes of meetings; and various layers of administrative complexity familiar to anyone who has run a small business or wrestled with the bureaucratic demands placed on arts bodies, or both.

We were also fortunate to have stories and information from a number of other poets who had and, in most cases, continue to maintain a strong connection with Friendly Street. Some of the people responsible for starting Friendly Street wrote to us and spoke about the early days and other aspects of Friendly Street. These included Richard Tipping, Andrew Taylor and Kate Llewellyn, whose warmth for Friendly Street is still clear. Apart from those already mentioned, we were also able to rely on input from more recently involved people such as Graham Catt, Louise Nicholas, Jude Aquilina, and Judy Dally. The strong commitment and enthusiasm for the success of Friendly Street was evident in all of their contributions and comments.

And lastly, our thanks must go to the many poets and members of the audience at hundreds of Friendly Street readings who have kept it lively, accessible, provocative, and always stimulating for more than thirty years. In 1982, Dennis Haskell remarked that, 'in recent years Adelaide's "Friendly Street" poets have been by far the best organised and most active group of poets in Australia'. That still rings true.

THE FIRST THIRTY YEARS
OF THE
FRIENDLY STREET POETS

AT THE BEGINNING

The history of Friendly Street is a story of poets seeing a need to create a performance space for poetry and doing something about it. Here is the background of Friendly Street and its activities: its genesis, its financial crisis, its successes as a publisher and organiser of Australia's longest running poetry performance venue, and more. Naturally, one begins at the beginning.

The first Friendly Street reading was held on a hot Tuesday night on 11th November 1975 – a date also memorable for the dismissal of the country's elected Labor government by the Governor General, Sir John Kerr. After the tumultuous events of the day, the poetry faithful met in what John Griffin called 'the intimate discomfort' and Carol Treloar described as 'the pokey upstairs screening room' of the Media Resource Centre in the former Gordon Sim Choon fireworks factory, which was located in Union Street in the commercial heart of Adelaide.

Some of the poets gathered on the roof of the building and looked out over the city, contemplating the future of a nation in political upheaval. John Bray, then the Chief Justice of South Australia, proclaimed that 'poetry is more important than politics'. Andrew Taylor, one of the originators of Friendly Street recalls:

> Standing on top of Gordon Choon's Fireworks Factory roof with John Bray, talking about the constitutional crisis and waiting until it was time to start the reading. The evening sun blazing, as it does in Adelaide. And we knew we were starting an experiment that just might work! Governments come and go, but poets go on forever.

Had they tried looking thirty years ahead, some of the poets at that first Friendly Street reading might have correctly predicted an increasingly conservative political climate and an ascendant economic rationalism. In Adelaide that night, though, as they drank red wine from flagons and listened to poetry being performed live, few would have foreseen that Friendly Street would be still running, let alone that it would by then have published more than 70 books, convened over 300 readings, helped to nurture the early writing careers of countless poets, and hold legitimate claim to being Australia's most significant series of poetry readings.

Why did Friendly Street happen? In part it was due to the mid-1960s growth in popular culture. People felt empowered to express themselves in numerous art forms, engaging with issues both of personal identity and the times in which they lived. According to critic James Tulip, poets a few years after the so-called 'generation of '68' became less connected to the particular styles in overseas writing – less inclined to follow American influences, especially – and there existed a fragmented but burgeoning activity in the arts across Australia. It sought a more local character and an individual voice on developing issues such as the Vietnam War and feminism.

Baby boomers had something to say and they wanted to be heard.

A greater literary awareness in Australia in the early 1970s was also signalled by the formation of the Australia Council and the Literature Board in 1973. The Labor Party had gained national government in 1972 and there was optimism that it might encourage a stronger sense of Australian identity through, among other things, the arts.

In Adelaide, the emergence of Friendly Street was a key expression of that desire for a regional gathering and sharing of poetic output. Andrew Taylor, Richard Tipping and Ian Reid were instrumental in getting Friendly Street going. They had returned from separate trips to the US and 'began asking why Adelaide did not have something like the small, public poetry readings which were so popular in the United States'. All three had seen how the poetry scene there was spreading out from its traditional places and to such venues as coffee shops and bookshops. Tipping said he was keen to see a similar diversity of reading sites. Further talk led to a planning meeting where, fortified by a spinach pie that Kate Llewellyn provided, these Adelaide poets plus a number of others (including Christine Churches, Nancy Gordon, John Griffin and Rob Johnson) discussed the idea of holding a new type of poetry reading.

Andrew Taylor remarks that in Adelaide, 'there was nothing involving younger people, and no place for beginners to come and hear, read and socialise. It was really a barren landscape – or, more accurately, it seemed to be barren until Friendly Street brought all the ongoing activity out into the open'. Tipping is regarded by the others as the one who named Friendly Street, though he does not recall doing so: he said Friendly Street was a name which simply started to be used, and suited the feeling of community that was being generated.

According to James Tulip, on the national scene, the work of David Malouf, Judith Rodriguez, Thomas Shapcott and Roger McDonald, in particular, had helped to 'consolidate and professionalise the core of their generation's writing' between 1965 and 1985. Through their various roles such as introducing poetry publication to the University of Queensland Press, poetry editing and criticism, and Shapcott's term as Chair of the Literature Board of the Australia Council, they assisted in lifting the profile of poetry. In Adelaide, as elsewhere at this time, poets looked for outlets where they could read and publish their work, and there was a proliferation of small literary magazines.

The initial fortnightly readings would settle into a monthly pattern (but for January) and a steady stream of readers and listeners would keep on coming. Taylor, Reid and Tipping were right; Friendly Street did meet a need. But could it sustain?

THE IMPORTANCE OF PLACE

The first site of the poetry meetings was the Media Resource Centre. Yet it was not the best fit for purpose because of the mixed uses to which it was put. It was primarily an exhibition space and during that first year of readings somehow a painting was damaged. The poets had to move. So, by 1976, Friendly Street shifted a few blocks south to the Federal Box Factory in Regent Street, where it was to stay for more than 20 years. An organisation can become identified with the place it inhabits, and that has certainly been true of Friendly Street. The Federal Box Factory, run by the Box Factory Community Centre, had been the long-term venue for a variety of community activities including Friendly Street's monthly readings, and was eventually regarded by many as the spiritual home of Friendly Street.

The Box Factory was so strongly identified with and by the Friendly Street group, that an image of the building was featured on the organisation's website and on the cover of more than one of its anthologies. The Box Factory was itself to prove never an ideal site, and a succession of Friendly Street committees were to consider the possibility of a change. As early as 1992 the premises of the newly formed South Australian Writers' Centre (SAWC), an umbrella body representing the interests of a number of writing organisations, were mooted as an alternative location. The issue would not die away. In 1998, the question of a possible move was again raised, principally due to complaints about a lack of both public phones and accessible public transport at night. The issue bubbled under for some time and the location of Friendly Street readings was to become a divisive issue.

In the Box Factory years, readings were initially held downstairs. This allowed direct access from the street, which explained the occasional unexpected visitor. Perhaps attracted by lights and other signs of life, strangers would wander in, listen for a while, and then settle down for the remainder of the night's readings. Some of them returned for another night of engaging poetry, and others for the free alcohol. The atmosphere was domestic, casual. You could imagine it was someone's welcoming living room. Battered armchairs and a sofa were bagsed first; they were more comfortable than the school chairs that could get hard.

There were frequently other activities being conducted on the upper floor during the poetry readings, at least for the early part of the evening. As they read their work, Friendly Street poets might have to contend with the overhead thumping of martial arts exponents or the exotic music of trainee belly dancers. Somehow, it seemed fitting for poetry to be in the mix like this, but it could make poetry reading difficult.

If no one else had booked the upper floor, and a bigger than normal crowd was expected for the Friendly Street reading, it was sometimes held in the larger space there. Later, when structural work was to be undertaken on the ground floor, Friendly Street was asked to shift all of its readings upstairs. Though it was a less confined area and better able to accommodate the growing audience, the atmosphere was different, and several poets lamented the change. Holding the readings upstairs also raised an equity issue because it made attendance virtually impossible for some disabled poets, so Friendly Street arranged to have every third reading downstairs. In 2002, Friendly Street supported the Box Factory Community Centre's request to the owner of the building, Adelaide City Council, for funding to install a lift, but that was unsuccessful.

A legislative ban on indoor smoking further altered the character of the readings, though the drinking continued. At the end of 2000, smoking was banned even on the outside balcony at the Box Factory, forcing smokers into the side-garden below, or onto the footpath (from where one could occasionally glimpse pairs of poets smooching in the car park). Aside from the valid health concerns about cigarettes, the ban meant the end of the characteristic smokers' gathering, one more element of the old Friendly Street disappearing – but then such changes were occurring in public spaces elsewhere, too.

In August 2003, the Council cut the Box Factory Committee's funding altogether and took over management of the Centre. The following month, it also closed the building on occupational health grounds, forcing Friendly Street to shift out on very short notice. Homeless, Friendly Street was offered temporary accommodation at the South Australian Writers' Centre by its director, Barbara Wiesner. For all the years of consideration to move to the heart of the city, here unexpectedly, poetic activity could be conducted. Worse news followed. Lockdown at the Box Factory continued and Friendly Street was denied access to its main stocks of poetry books. Suddenly a major form of income for the organisation was denied. Despite pleas, the Council would not allow access to the building and would give no commitment that the Box Factory would ever again be available. This uncertainty cast a shadow over Friendly Street that produced tensions between many people, often directed at members of the committee.

The Friendly Street committee was vigilant in its efforts to explore all options for a venue. It investigated more than a dozen alternative sites, eventually presenting detailed findings and a short list of three locations to a rather stormy Annual General Meeting. There were strong arguments on both sides and the debate was heated. The most common objection to permanently leaving the Box Factory for the SA Writers' Centre was that Friendly Street would lose its independence by being under the same roof as other writing bodies used, and there were also questions over access, venue size, parking, and various matters. Even with a vote narrowly favouring a further three-month trial of the SA Writers' Centre (26 against 23), some people were clearly reluctant to adapt to the change. One committee member complained that he had been bailed up on the night by an emotional Friendly Street character of long-standing and accused of a conflict of interest since he was also on the board of the Writers' Centre. He wrote an aggrieved seven-page letter to his colleagues on the Friendly Street Committee about the ordeal.

When the City Council eventually cleared the way for a possible return to the Box Factory, another round of arguments ensued between Friendly Street members about the merits of returning. It was decided not to go back, but there were at least two more occasions, one as late as the 2006 AGM, when the case for moving back to the Box Factory was informally put to the members.

Perhaps the issue still simmers, but in this last instance there was only lukewarm response to reviving the matter. In any case, all of the discussions seem to have been open and democratic, two principles firmly in accord with the philosophies of Friendly Street. Some regulars have only ever known the SA Writers' Centre as Friendly Street's venue. That hails from the old Malcolm Reid Furniture store, gutted and resurrected as offices above a ground floor of shops and cafés. Here, poetry meetings are not held inside the air-conditioned internal offices, but in the larger atrium. This interesting space has a clear roof and suspended sail curtains. Radiating from the centre of the space is a relic of the merchant past – a flying fox network of wires that once sent canisters with money and dockets over the heads of customers. The site feels worlds away from the Box Factory's ground or first floor venues. Some feel, though, a ghost of the Box Factory haunts the monthly meetings. Perhaps it is only the wine.

MAKING IT INTO THE BOOK

Some people could not, or feigned not, to understand the naming of Friendly Street. According to Don Anderson: 'This seemed a misnomer, if not an oxymoron ... Poetry readings were the nearest thing Australia had to a blood sport'. So what is a Friendly Street reading really like? Well, there have been fights, and there has been abuse and the occasional throwing of objects.

But these events are not usual ...

When the venue is first opened for the night's reading, there is usually a group of waiting people keen to see the Book put out. The Book is where intending readers write their names, so it governs the order of reading. There have been three of these over the years, and in each volume one can trace who was chairing the meeting, who read their poetry, and who was a guest reader.

Poets who arrive early might leave the first few lines of the page empty, so they can get a feel for the way the audience is reacting before it is their turn to face the crowd. On the other hand, there have been many times when someone who did not arrive early enough would find so many other names already listed that he or she would be unlikely to be called for hours. A little negotiation might ensue, with appeals to the night's MC to allow them to move up the list, but the order usually holds. There are only a few mentions in the minutes of the Friendly Street Committee of anyone complaining about such 'pushing in'. Anecdotally it might be different.

At a Friendly Street reading, there is time for a general gossip and catching up while the room is being organised for the night's affairs. Chairs are brought out and arranged, and the sound system is set up, and so on, before the first poet is called. The flavour of Friendly Street readings has changed over time but the core of the night's activity remains essentially the same, offering a mix of open reading and one or two featured poets. Some people choose to emphasise the theatrical potential of their poetry but the norm is to simply stand and read – not that this is always an easy thing. As for the standard of the poetry itself, Graham Rowlands once remarked that, 'the quality of the work ... ranges from the occasionally appalling to the occasional masterpiece'.

Peter Porter, who once appeared at Friendly Street as a guest reader, wrote: 'it seems that poetry is doomed to never become a spectator sport, but always a practitioner's'. Perhaps he didn't get to enough poetry readings like those at Friendly Street, which could be tough going at times and always offered the chance of a poet making a spectacle of him or herself. Readings were generally boisterous in the Box Factory days, partly due to greater consumption of alcohol, but there are still many spiky moments, and many innovative performances, at contemporary Friendly Street readings.

Mike Ladd credits Friendly Street with making space for theatrical elements in the reading of poetry: 'Friendly Street has really encouraged poets to lift their game in performing their work. It's generally been open to different types of performances'. Poets have read while standing on tables, or while crouching under them. Various people have employed music: Richard Tipping liked to play a kalimba or ukulele or jaw harp during his readings; Mike Ladd has used recordings of drums and played a video poem; Geoff Hastwell often pulls out his guitar; and the talented Avalanche (aka Ivan Rehorek) commonly arrives at the mike with a flourish from one of the many instruments he plays, and leaves in the same way.

Joint readings have sometimes deliberately blurred the authorship of the work, such as with Jan Owen and Steve Evans. Khail Juredeini has read his poems while dressed in a silver space suit. Poets have been nailed into boxes and smashed their way out of them. Nancy Gordon conducted readings while wearing a top hat, and Richard Tipping once used a starting pistol as a way of warning that poets had gone over time.

There have been multicultural readings, both as programmed events and as ad hoc translations. It has been quite a variety of performances. One way or another, there have been numerous embellishments to the evenings at Friendly Street, and there is no way to know beforehand what might unfold before the audience.

THROWING JEWELLERY AND WINE

Reading a poem out loud, and especially in public, adds a different dimension. One can enjoy the sound and rhythm of the work, its pauses and changes of pace. The poet might suddenly hear where a poem needs further work, or adjust the reading of it to the occasion and the nature of the crowd. Reading aloud may also add another ingredient to the mix – fear!

It can be confronting for a poet, not least because it is such an immediate experience. The audience is right in front of you, and mistakes can't be rewound or edited out. Some poets have read despite an attack of nerves that means they can't even hear their own voices, but a poet who perseveres through that stage acquires a new and vital connection to his or her writing.

Friendly Street actively welcomes and celebrates new-comers. First-time readers are supposed to announce their novice status, and receive a round of applause before they read. Such support comes simply for having the courage to begin this very public exposure of their craft. The more a poet reads his or her work in public, the more attuned they become to their poetry, and the better it is.

In a review of one Friendly Street anthology, Christopher Pollnitz praised the 'rigorous principles on which [poets] select poems to be read before a live audience'. Other reviewers, such as John McLaren and Heather Cam (formerly Johnstone) have also referred to the discipline involved in public reading as contributing to the quality of poems in the annual antholo-gies, the Readers.

Poets are reluctant to give up an opportunity to read. The Friendly Street Committee initially set a finishing time, which meant that on busier nights some people on the list would face a real risk of missing out. The committee tried limiting the time allocated to the individual poets, following a tendency by some people to read until audience grumbling set in. A ten-minute cap was trialled, which was then reduced to five minutes, but there were still so many would-be readers that this too was soon under attack. By 1992, readers had only three minutes apiece, with long poems to be left for the end of the night if there was still time, an arrangement that has essentially survived.

At the time of writing (2007), the format for a typical evening at Friendly Street is to start the open readings at 7:00pm with the first half a dozen poets who have signed on being asked to perform their work. After this, one or two guest readers take the floor for about fifteen minutes each. Then there are various announcements (forthcoming reading functions and book launches) and, on some nights, there is a promotional spot for the author of a new collection to read for up to five minutes. A break follows. This is when books are bought, gossip is sought and relayed, drinks are consumed, networking is undertaken, praise is given and received, and questions and debates are raised.

After twenty minutes or so, the open readings are resumed. If the sign-on list is long, the remaining poets might have to suffer a reduced reading time or a more severe limit on the number of poems. If such a cut is announced partway through the night, it can be frustrating to those further down the list. A poet who has arrived with three quite short poems, for instance, may still find their spot restricted to just one poem. Readings now extend from a previous closing time of 10:30pm to almost midnight. It means that the Friendly Street patrons get to hear a couple of guest poets plus something like 50 or 60 others airing their work.

Friendly Street has not always been as friendly as its name suggests. Exciting or thematically challenging material can incite a reaction from an audience, and there have been a number of altercations. Feedback is usually couched with humour but at times it can also be less than generous. Mike Ladd recalls:

> Sometimes when an excruciating poem was being read, the heckling was the most interesting thing to listen to. Or during the height of '70s feminism, there would be a chorus of hisses when some bumbling male (accidentally or otherwise) read out a chauvinist line. You really had to careful – I remember one guy getting crucified for reading a poem about sex, which used a ploughing metaphor – BAD CHOICE!

It wasn't always the men on the receiving end; for better or worse, some of them played tough as well. When Kate Jennings read 'sad and angry poems' from her collection, *Come to Me My Melancholy Baby*, in the early days, Carol Treloar recalls that, 'you could have cut the air . . . the reaction was extreme, very emotional. There were mutterings, jeers, visible squirmings (from a few men!), but there were also moving statements of support and praise and gratitude.' While opinions may vary on just how Jennings was received that night, it was definitely a strong response. According to Moya Costello, there were nights in the 1980s when heckling threatened to overwhelm the poetry as some of the audience, especially the men, vied for attention.

Heather Cam says that 'to attend a poetry performance is to be part of a social occasion and a participant in a living art form'. She remembers the impact that one Friendly Street character had on some of the poets:

> You ran the gauntlet of 'commentary' from Old Snow, an inebriated regular ensconced at the back, who trained a generation of Friendly Street Poets in the art of keeping tuned to the audience; they learned smartly enough the peril of being boring, pretentious or inept.

It was Snow who, after only ever tossing loud, one-word criticisms over the heads of the audience, surprised everyone one night by signing up to read. When his name was called he walked slowly to the long counter at the front of the room, carrying his usual cane shopping basket over one arm. He deposited the basket on the bench and proceeded to carefully unwrap a series of crumpled pieces of paper, silently examine each one, and then replace it. Finally, he lingered over one such scrap and looked at us: 'I am ... nothing,' he said. He balled the piece of paper tightly, thrust it back into the basket, and resumed his place at the back of the room without a further word.

Regular Friendly Street goers of longstanding may remember other dramatic episodes from the earlier years. Once when a poet would not respond to repeated calls to end his reading, Kate Llewellyn grabbed the only thing she could think of at the time, her heavy and valuable silver bracelet, and threw it at him. According to Llewellyn, he promptly took off into the night with her jewellery, followed by several people who finally caught him and retrieved it.

Mike Ladd remembers another occasion that also features in several poets' recollections:

There were some fiery nights in the Box Factory. Once, when I happened to be MC, an interstate poet refused to stop reading long after his time was up. He'd taken up 20 minutes in the open reading spot ... I asked him to stop, but he wouldn't. We then took a vote, and he lost, though there were some in the audience who wanted him to keep going because it was anarchic. He still refused to go, saying something like 'the performance space is sacred'. A shouting debate started. Then I then found myself in the middle of a wrestling match, when Andrew Taylor, normally a very peaceful bloke, tried to drag the poet from the stage. We were then doused in red flagon wine by Beate Josephi

[Taylor's wife], who broke up the melee, and the guy stormed off into the night, cursing, swearing and dripping cheap plonk.

The launches of the annual anthologies, collections known as Readers, have been enlivened by various incidents over the years. At one, a rather worse for wear publisher was reclining on an old lounge suite at the back of the room and began loudly heckling a poet, eventually calling for her to, 'Shut up, you wrinkled old twat!' – not initially realising it was one of his own authors. When told of the connection, the publisher laughed, 'Well . . . she's terrible!'

In 1980, Graham Rowlands presided over the launch of Reader Number 4 while dressed as Ned Kelly. Wearing an overcoat and with a metal bucket as a helmet, he sat brandishing a rifle for the first part of the evening. At the launch of Reader Number 7, the cover designer, Casey Van Sebille, claimed that his work was also a poem and proceeded to 'read it out'.

There would be a call for announcements at half time, during which Rowlands often held his bargain sales, usually of literary journals in which his work had just appeared (and there were many of those). He also held competitions for poems on particular themes, with prizes that he donated, such as an oil painting or a bottle of wine.

These events were the kind of spice one might expect when so many people gathered in a hot room with plenty of alcohol and a determination to assert their artistic talent. Friendly Street is an organisation that prides itself on its inclusive nature, and any upsets were mostly of the forgive-and-forget kind, sporadic and amusing in their way. Perhaps people became more conservative over the years, but there were ructions in the early 1990s when some heckling had become barbed and there were angry exchanges. The Friendly Street Committee was so concerned about the disruptive behaviour that in April 1992 it devised a policy for dealing with them, and announced it at the following month's reading. A single warning, if unheeded, would result in the miscreants being permanently barred. How they might actually enforce the policy was another matter.

Interruptions since that period have been generally fewer and seldom malicious. These days, one need not avoid reading at Friendly Street for fear of jewellery being thrown or wine hurled, but interjections can still occur. The latest fuss has been about whether there is a right to read pornographic poetry, and that has polarised the Friendly Street crowd. Like a political party in melt-down, will the group split along party lines? Perhaps, but if the past is a guide, Friendly Street will ride out the issue.

Through the years, though, there have also been cheers, dancing, chants, sing-alongs, a lot of laughter, and many moments of silent awe at the beauty or daring of the poetry.

ADVOCACY AND LOCAL PUBLISHING

Friendly Street is the closest thing that South Australia has to an advocacy body for poets and poetry. Many years ago this was the preserve of the branches of the Poets Union, which began in South Australia in 1978, just before its national body was founded. The SA branch was claimed to be the most successful and vigorous in the country. Its local members provided much of the organisation for the Friendly Street readings, and both Jenny Boult and Kate Llewellyn held office as its national secretary for some time. The Poets Union held local readings, timed not to clash with those of Friendly Street, and flourished in the state until 1985 when the SA Writers' Centre was established.

The SA Writers' Centre, though it had many Friendly Street people on its board, of course represented more genres than poetry. The new state-wide advocate took up the broad issues associated with being a writer in numerous fields. While the Poets Union has since ceased in South Australia, it is still going strong in NSW as a national body representing the interests of poets and poetry, albeit with a centre of gravity clearly located in the eastern states.

In some ways, the SA branch of the Poets Union is arguably the predecessor of today's Friendly Street Poets Association Inc., having had similar activities, people, and aims. At least its goals have been conflated with those of Friendly Street itself. The general objects of the Friendly Street constitution include: 'to foster, promote and encourage the reading, reciting and publication of poetry' [Friendly Street Poets Incorporated Constitution: 3.1 Objects]. Though its more visible activities primarily revolve around the readings and publishing program, it has never lost sight of this general goal of promoting poetry.

In 1992, for example, Friendly Street sent poet (and now novelist) James Bradley to a Poetrylink Conference in Sydney, with financial support from the Department for the Arts and Cultural Heritage (these days known as Arts SA). The conference was intended to establish active poetry advocacy groups in each state that would be able to operate collectively when necessary. They were meant to constitute a National Poets Association, and each issue of a magazine, *OzMuse*, would carry news on their events. *OzMuse* was shortlived, however, and while the Poets Union still agitates for poetry being given more respect, it is Friendly Street that carries the banner in South Australia.

Could it do more to help local poetry?

Opportunities can be tantalisingly close and ideas can promise a great deal, without ever being realised. Friendly Street was invited to send a representative to the Performing Arts Annual Congress in Sydney in 2001 but its budget did not allow this. In 2002, it applied for funding to enable someone to concentrate on advocacy and the coordination of poetry activities in South Australia, but again this depended on the level of the next grant from Arts SA, which turned out to be insufficient.

As it is, Friendly Street achieves a great deal with the funding it receives, essentially because of the many hours of volunteer work by its committee members.

The Friendly Street Committee has been keen to see publishing opportunities for SA poets extend beyond its own program. For instance, the lack of space provided for poetry in the local daily newspaper, *The Advertiser*, has been a disappointment for many years. John Griffin, one of the early driving forces behind Friendly Street, had briefly been able to get South Australian writers' poems into the paper, one at a time. Afterwards, Friendly Street made sporadic offers to edit submissions for free if the paper would make a small space available for poetry, but without success. As Graham Rowlands says, 'neither flattery nor rudeness will place your poem in *The Advertiser*'.

Complaints to the paper were routinely ignored, with the exception of local poet Glen Murdoch, who went right to the top with his complaint, addressing it to the paper's owner. According to Rowlands, he got a 'long, charming letter explaining the absence of poetry ... written by none other than the Deputy Editor', presumably because Glen had written to Rupert Murdoch and 'someone had concluded that the only person capable of pestering Rupert about poetry had to be a relative'.

Another opportunity has been the free Adelaide monthly paper, *The Adelaide Review*. It received funding from the Australia Council to publish original writing but largely preferred a small group of writers of whom only one, Peter Goldsworthy, was South Australian. Les Murray and Peter Porter did well out of it. The Friendly Street Committee sought a change in the *Review*'s editorial stance but there were very few exceptions to the paper's previous practice. For a while, the Committee bought space in the *Review* to advertise Friendly Street activities and publish a poem that had been read at Friendly Street. Ralph Bleechmore submitted advertising copy to *The Adelaide Review* for the August 1990 reading that included the final line: 'Sponsored by: 'Access-by-a-wider-range-of-poets-to-the-Adelaide-Review-poetry-page-group.' We don't know whether the advertisement eventually appeared with those words but it doesn't seem likely.

There have been other places in South Australia to which one might send poetry apart from newspapers. *Southern Review*, once a journal of the University of Adelaide, published poetry to a small readership. *Fields: a poetry magazine* appeared, for just a few issues only, in the 1970s, as did *Ash*, Larry Buttrose's *Dharma*, and *Real Poetry*. In the late 1970s, John Griffin was responsible for editing a free poetry flyer, *Poems Public*, which was distributed in Adelaide's CBD and elsewhere. For a while in the early 1980s, an art and literature magazine, *Words and Visions*, was available. Ken Bolton's fat literary magazine, *Otis Rush*, also offered a prospect of publication within its own editorial style. None of these is a functioning South Australian publication now*.

In the late 1990s, Martin Johnson persuaded *The Bunyip*, Gawler's newspaper serving towns to the north of Adelaide, to do what *The Advertiser* had abandoned, and it actually paid the poets whose work was published. Sadly, that opportunity also did not last though during the period of Martin's poetry page many poets enjoyed seeing their work in news print, with the added bonus that the northern community had the pleasure of seeing contemporary poetry in its local paper.

A handful of publishing opportunities continue. Cath Keneally on Radio Adelaide, formerly called Radio 5UV, still broadcasts local poets. Radio National's *Poetica*, run by Mike Ladd from the station's Adelaide studio sometimes does this as well, though it has an understandably country-wide interest. Arts SA's own bi-monthly publication, *Art State*, features poems selected by the editors of each forthcoming Friendly Street anthology from the work read at the previous monthly meeting. It's a good-looking glossy and having a whole page dedicated to Friendly Street poets is a coup. One spark of excitement is the new Adelaide newspaper, the *Independent Weekly*, whose in-house poetry editor, John Miles, has a Poet's Corner. An enthusiastic promoter of poetry, he draws submissions from Friendly Street and beyond. Sadly, however, poets can't always expect payment for their art.

The state's tertiary educational institutions with their burgeoning writing programs are doing their bit for publication, too. Roger Zubrinich at the Adelaide Centre for the Arts (ACA) supported editor Lachlan Colquhoun's handsome *Post Taste* magazine that featured students like Pat Irvine. She, like other Professional Writing graduates John De Laine and Jude Aquilina, gained publication in New Poets or Single

---

* A fuller explanation of the publishing scene up to 1990 can be found in *Tuesday Night Live: Fifteen Years of Friendly Street.*

Poet collections, and became firm Friendly Street regulars. Phillip Edmonds at the University of Adelaide seed funded the creative writing journal, *Wet Ink*, which provides some space and payment for poems. Ioana Petrescu continues to increase the University of South Australia's involvement in publishing and editing poetry ventures and one of its writing program's postgraduate students, Cameron Fuller, published his first collection through Friendly Street. Jeri Kroll, long-time Friendly Street author, is the program director of the new Bachelor of Creative Arts and supervisor for doctoral poetry students at Flinders University. Such activities can only increase the vigour of Friendly Street publishing.

What is undeniable is the efforts of the Friendly Street Committee to keep publishing ongoing, even through indirect effects. Without an active poetry community supported by Friendly Street, much of the impetus for publication might have withered. What cannot be forgotten is that Friendly Street has its own publishing program – that highlights the effort and quality of the region's poets – whether they are regular, metropolitan, student or rural scribes.

Friendly Street contributes more than just pushing for the publication of poetry, it involves itself in lots of associated activities and contributes to local communities, bringing the word of the poet into the heart of suburbia.

Friendly Street has done a lot to foster poetry through its involvement in the Spring Poetry Festivals, the Marion Learning Festivals, and National Poetry Week activities. It has also conducted poetry competitions that raise the profile of poetry in South Australia. The most prominent of these is the Satura Prize, which is funded by a bequest from the estate of John Bray. His will stipulated that the money was 'to be used in such manner as it shall in its absolute discretion think fit for the benefit of poetry or poets in South Australia', and it rewards the author of the poem that a South Australian identity judges to be the best in the latest Reader. Distinguished judges have included two SA State Governors, two SA Premiers, a Federal Senator, the Lord Mayor of Adelaide, and a Nobel Prize winner, J M Coetzee.

Other competitions include two prizes that Friendly Street offers for school students in the South Australian English Teachers' Association Spring Poetry Festival, and the Nova Prize for the best new poet to appear in the latest Reader. More recently established prizes have been for the best political poem and the best mystical poem in the newest Reader.

Various Friendly Street Committees would have liked better results in their advocacy role, especially in respect of the local press supporting poetry by publishing and reviewing it. In the face of such intransigence, perhaps the best policy is to campaign for change while embracing a do-it-yourself approach, as Friendly Street has done since 1976. Given some of the events in its history, it's sometimes hard to believe how Friendly Street did come to prosper as a publisher of poetry.

POETS AS PUBLISHERS –
A CHANGING DYNAMIC

Looking back at the publishing record of Friendly Street, one could easily mistake its constant output for the sign of a larger and confident commercial operation. Friendly Street has provided a continuous reading venue since 1975 and published an annual Reader since 1977, with additional volumes being added later on a regular basis. It was not planned this way, but there were forces at work that seemed to make the opportunity irresistible. The publishing environment into which Friendly Street ventured was one that had turned sour for a number of poets, even those of considerable reputation, when federal support for the arts had waned. The extensive list of Friendly Street books masks some real difficulties that have threatened to derail its own publishing activities several times.

The Adelaide University Union Press published the first three Friendly Street Readers, but then the press closed. As Jeri Kroll noted in her *Writers' Radio* program, South Australia then had 'no substantial press publishing much creative work, especially poetry'. At this time, Graham Rowlands made the point that many Friendly Street poets had extensive publication acknowledgements to show, yet Angus & Robertson or the University of Queensland Press and their like were not publishing their individual collections. It was an issue that many South Australian poets, even those with national reputations, were pondering. Friendly Street, through its focus on a local publishing program, would help to redress the imbalance.

The Friendly Street Collective, comprising a number of Adelaide poets, was formed in 1980 to issue *Friendly Street Reader 4*, and it continued through to the twelfth volume as a Readers' Sub-committee from 1981. In that period, typesetting and printing was contracted to the University Relations Unit at Flinders University. The Collective's activity was essential given waning government support for the publication of poetry in Australia. In 1982, social historian and commentator, Humphrey McQueen, wrote:

> Ten years ago, books of poetry were being published by commercial firms supported by the Literature Board. In the past six years, the money springs have dried up and several commentators have become downhearted and are now crying woe over the condition of the arts in Australia ... If we are concerned about the decline in Australian writing, is it because we are looking in the wrong places and with the wrong expectations about the way a culture proceeds?

McQueen went on to applaud the emergence of alternative 'energy sources', notably small presses, and Friendly Street's publishing program in particular as a logical response to the lack of funding from government.

Poets on the Friendly Street Collective at various times included Larry Buttrose, Peter Goldsworthy, Nancy Gordon, Rory Harris, Jeri Kroll, Kate Llewellyn, Kevin Pearson and Graham Rowlands. It was this sub-committee that, with assistance from the SA Arts Grants Advisory Committee, 'organised printers, typesetters, designers, publicity and distribution'. It also devised and documented guidelines to help make the publication of successive Readers more professional by standardising some key layout and design elements. It was not all smooth running, however. Rowlands, in particular, expended considerable energy trying to get bookshops to stock Friendly Street titles. They were often reluctant to do so, despite the existence of very good reviews. Those reviews were almost entirely from interstate because, frustratingly (and strangely), Adelaide's own daily newspapers were not interested in local poetry. Efforts continued in the hope of persuading *The Advertiser* to review poetry more frequently but things in Adelaide have hardly improved in this regard since Friendly Street began.

For the first few years there was just the annual anthology, capturing the spirit and the best quality of the year's readings. Under the arrangements devised by the Friendly Street Collective, individual poets' collections had also been published. Publishing the latter required the authors to provide a guarantee against loss (a potential maximum cost of $3000–$4000 each) in case a sufficient external subsidy did not materialise. This was simply a cautious act by the committee, but it meant that two poets withdrew manuscripts that otherwise stood to be published. Such funding was never a sure thing and the risk of financial burden would have weighed heavily on the minds of some writers, especially those with limited resources. Until at least the fourth series of individual collections, the poets still had to provide such a guarantee. In any case, it turned out that the government grants were sufficient for this condition not to be invoked.

Poets did take the risk and helped to establish Friendly Street as a premier publisher of solo collections alongside its annual Readers. Between 1982 and 1988, Friendly Street launched five books at each Writers' Week; it was a sizeable output and one that was not expected from a fledgling publisher. Rowlands orchestrated the original publishing and distribution with Flinders Press and the program seemed to run well. The Readers were commended for their production values, eliciting comments such as 'exceptionally well-produced book' (Geoffrey Dutton) and 'very handsome' (Frank Kellaway).

The funding increased, but for a community program run by volunteers money-handling could be problematic. Without adequate restraints, checks or balances, it was a disaster waiting to happen.

In 1988, just when Friendly Street had real momentum in its publishing program and there was a growing national respect for it, a large amount of Friendly Street funds were embezzled – and further government funding was withheld.

The confidence of Friendly Street regulars was shaken, and the future of its publishing activities suddenly looked grim. The shock of financial trouble was to change the way books would be published. Two years later, Friendly Street would set up an arrangement with local publishing house, Wakefield Press, and new government support would be made available. These money woes represented an important threat to the ambitions of Friendly Street publishing as well as to its other activities, and repercussions would be felt ever more.

Friendly Street books, and the successive Readers in particular, are public evidence of the standard of the monthly readings. It is critical then to maintain not just the quality of their content but also to make them visually attractive, and to do so within a realistic budget that will get the books into the public eye. Naturally then, Friendly Street has periodically revisited how it should run its publishing activities, including the nature of its relationship with Wakefield Press. There are other firms capable of producing books, of course, and the Friendly Street Committee has weighed up additional aspects such as marketing and distribution of its titles. When, in 1992, the Department for the Arts and Cultural Heritage wrote that it expected Friendly Street to generate more income through better distribution, Friendly Street seemed to have anticipated this criticism – it had just revised its co-publishing and distribution deal with Wakefield Press.

In 1992, Friendly Street published two volumes that each combined the work of three poets, *Three's Company* and *Across the Gulf.* Soon afterwards, it was proposed that Friendly Street launch a number of slim volumes (30 pages) by individual poets, referred to as 'new presentation poetry booklets', and in 1994 it called for manuscripts. These stapled titles would have been virtually invisible on bookshop shelves, however, which led the Committee back to the successful three-in-one format. Thus, Friendly Street formally began its New Poets series that allows short manuscripts by three poets to be published in a combined volume, showcasing the work of people who have not previously had a full collection. The role of nurturing early-career writers would be reflected in a distinct part of the Friendly Street publishing spectrum, and Friendly Street titles would attract a wider readership. Submissions to the publications program come from all over the state, and the program has also used established poets as manuscript assessors, both aspects adding to the sense of this being a community operation.

In 1995 there was apprehension when it was rumoured that Wakefield Press was to stop publishing poetry altogether. Fortunately, that was not the case, but it gave the Committee reason to review its policy on publishing and distribution of Friendly Street titles, in order to obtain a better reach. As this volume attests, the relationship with Wakefield Press has survived all of the ups and downs. So far.

FRIENDLY STREET AT WRITERS' WEEK

In even-numbered years, Friendly Street still has a publishing peak that coincides with Writers' Week in the biennial Adelaide Festival of Arts. Since 1982, Friendly Street has used that occasion to launch its latest titles. It is a busy period, which gathers writers of national and international acclaim before a large audience, and Friendly Street is able to position itself for maximum publicity. In 1984 Judith Rodriguez remarked that Adelaide's Friendly Street Poets set an entrepreneurial example to other regional publishers, by launching its books at the Festival. This is not done purely for commercial advantage, though that helps – it also reminds a large audience of literary fans and some journalists that Adelaide has a vigorous poetry scene with a very well respected publishing output, and it allows people who do not attend the readings to understand what it is about. This has been very successful, with one or two hitches.

In 2002, stocks of all the freshly launched Friendly Street books were quickly exhausted at Writers' Week and, when new copies finally did arrive, the site's one official bookseller was slow to put them out for would-be buyers to look at. Agitated Friendly Street Committee members and many other poets wrung their hands in agitation at lost sales and exposure. The New Poets sat outside the book tent for their moment of glory to sign copies of their first collection of poetry only to have no books to be sold and none to sign.

In 2004, Friendly Street Convenor, David Adès, writing an acquittal report to Arts SA, remarked on the Writers' Week launch this way: 'In a step setting a new benchmark in ambition for Friendly Street publications, the editors of the *Friendly Street Reader* managed to secure the participation of the high profile Clive James in launching the book. It is unfortunate that his launch did not do the book justice'. Adès was being polite.

Clive James arrived at the very last minute and without

a copy of the new book. He initially said he had not been provided with one, even though it had been delivered to his hotel days before as requested. His personal assistant then blamed the hotel for not getting it to her before James arrived at the launch venue, and so it went. In any event, he glanced at the anthology behind the tent in which he was just about to speak, but without actually reading any poem. When he assumed the stage, he proceeded to talk about himself for the duration of the session.

One bright spot was the announcement of the inaugural Nova prize to the best first-time published Friendly Street poet. Genuinely surprised at his success, documentary film-maker Rob de Kok walked from the back row of the West Tent to receive his award. 'Writing poetry is like ripping open your chest and pulling out your heart,' de Kok said from the podium. His few words into the mike rivetted the audience already gob-smacked at James' reading of his own long poem. It was a memorable launch.

Another regular part of the Writers' Week activities has been the Poets on Popeye readings, run by the SA Writers' Centre. These elegant affairs involve local poets reading along-side interstate and overseas poets from the Writers' Week program. One of the tourist cruise-boats, collectively known as Popeye, is loaded with a paying audience who listen to selected poets as they travel the River Torrens at dusk. Champagne is sipped and snacks nibbled. The local poets for each evening are typically drawn from the Friendly Street community of writers and it is a gig that is highly prized. You never know which famous overseas poet with whom you might be sharing the mike. It can be productive, or at least scintillating for all concerned. And the scenery is so very tranquil, unlike the hurly burly of the festival tents.

THE ANTHOLOGIES

The Friendly Street anthologies have been well received from the outset, though not without occasional criticism. John Griffin recognised the importance of the readings themselves when he reviewed the first volume, *The Friendly Street Poetry Reader*: 'Just about everyone who writes poetry in Adelaide got there at least once and there were plenty of listeners. It was a good audience, sympathetically providing feedback on what is heard'. Frank Kellaway described that book as 'one of the best anthologies covering about a year's poetry which I've seen' and Christopher Pollnitz enjoyed the first Reader for its liveliness and its quality.

Looking at *Number Two Friendly Street* (1978), Geoffrey Dutton wrote: 'By no means restricted to Adelaide poets, in its informal way *Friendly Street* has probably done more for poetry in Australia than any other group'. This is a large call, but an early sign of the importance of the new series of readings and their publishing output. Christopher Pollnitz noted 'the same diversity of styles and range of preoccupations ... as in eastern states volumes, with the difference that in Adelaide the poets seem able to co-exist amicably between the same covers'. Friendly by name ... By the time the eighth Reader emerged, there were proselytising reviews: 'The poetry is of a uniformly high standard ... I urge those readers who believe that Australian poetry ends with Paterson and Wright to look for this book' (Peter Lugg).

At the start, Richard Tipping chose to reflect the arbitrariness of the live readings by presenting the published poems in alphabetical order, and it is a policy with which almost all subsequent editors have stuck. The editorial process necessarily eliminates some good work. On the other hand, it has been made clear since the beginning that no one is guaranteed publication just because they read their work at Friendly Street.

Material selected for the Readers could not hope to capture the whole zest and timing of some of the more dramatically read poems. If the virtues of live poetry can never be accurately translated to the page, at least the Readers provide evidence that the poets' judicious selection of poems for performance at Friendly Street and, subsequently, editors' choices can still produce books that satisfy. That has been the double value of the Reader – preserving something of the feel of the readings during the year, and constituting a book of poetry that stands as an attractive volume independent of its live-reading origins.

It is a familiar refrain that publishing is a cosy club, guarded by a small group who look after their friends to the detriment of others. Similar claims from those who fail to get their work into a Friendly Street anthology are very rare, but they have occurred. In 1995, a flyer was distributed at a reading that questioned the timing of choices for the Festival year launch, the secrecy of assessment, the submission of manuscripts using pseudonyms, and the alleged reluctance of the Committee to discuss any of these matters. The flyer, which still sits in the Friendly Street files, was signed: 'Published in the interests of Friendly St. by the Committee for Democracy, Openess (*sic*) Motherhood and Ethics. (D.O.M.E.)' – sadly, no record of a reply is held there.

Some poets do want their spot in the Reader regardless, though, thinking that paying the door charge at a Friendly Street monthly reading automatically entitles them to be published. In 2002, one poet wrote to the Friendly Street Committee, complaining 'that regular F.S. attendees who pay their entry fee feel disgruntled because they are subsidising publication of other attendees' poems and that they have the right to have their poems published too ... I speak for a number of older, disgruntled, regular women attendees'. As was explained to the unhappy poet in this case, the entry fee is not levied to fund the publishing, and that each year's editors base their selections on issues of quality and balance. The $2 entry fee only recently increased to $4, then $5, and it does include cask red or white wine and soft drink options. Good value for money! Still, there are some other people who refuse to pay the door charge on principle, seeing it as antithetical to the essentially liberal spirit of Friendly Street – and perhaps also because they like to indulge in a little wishful thinking about the supposedly dissident nature of poets in general.

Being a newcomer is not necessarily an impediment to being published; a solid proportion of poets in each Reader has never been published by Friendly Street before. They often comprise over 20%, and sometimes close to 25% of the poets, demonstrating how well Friendly Street introduces new faces. In November 1993, Friendly Street through Glen Murdoch hosted a reading at the Boltz Café in Rundle Street East. Most of the people attending had never been to Friendly Street before and were generally younger than the usual Friendly Street crowd. More Nuts at Boltz readings followed, with the double advantage of bringing poetry readings to a new audience and connecting many of those poets to the regular Friendly Street readings. Offshoot readings continue to attract new poets, who would not be expected to rely on any prior acquaintance with the Friendly Street editors in getting their work selected. In any case, a new editorial team is brought in each year.

Many poets whose first collections were published by Friendly Street have gone on to release subsequent volumes. This has been quite marked where they first had a collection in the New Poets series, which combines the work of three poets. Friendly Street has acted as a launching pad for poets, whether their work has been brought to wider public attention via that series or through individual collections.

What else recommends the Friendly Street Readers, beyond capturing two editors' idea of the best of one year's poems? Susan McKernan in *The Canberra Times*, praised the value of the Readers as 'a welcome antidote to literary snobbery ... which provides publication for a range of writers and (gives) readers a chance to find the poetry they like best.' Just how the editors select work for each new Reader is perhaps still a mystery to many people, as the protests mentioned above seem to suggest. If you thought that you knew the writing of the editors in question, you might have tried to second-guess their tastes in others' work. One pair of editors did issue a broad guide to intending contributors, but it was mostly about what they did *not* like.

Studying the Friendly Street files showed up only two complaints about what was selected and rejected by editors of the anthologies, both from the same person. Either most people have been happy with the process or not so disaffected as to put their thoughts into words. In our review of the first thirty annual Readers, it seems impossible to gauge any clear similarity between the editors' own style of poetry and the poems they eventually selected. This at least indicates that the process of selection is broadly based.

Publishing the annual Readers has thrown up a couple of different and interesting problems, perhaps most notably with *No. 12 Friendly Street Poetry Reader.* The 1988 anthology's cover art so offended its editors, Jeff Guess and Donna McSkimming, that Guess said he would seek legal advice. The design featured somewhat plasticised representations of torsos and genitalia. The Friendly Street Committee issued a tongue-in-cheek press release announcing a voluntary recall: those who had already purchased the book would be entitled to claim a free brown-paper cover to hide the offending images. The book was also to be re-launched with its new look. However playful the response, there was real concern underlying the announcement. Production of that anthology had been the responsibility of Graham Rowlands and Kevin Pearson, who claimed that the editors had shown no real interest in the design and other production aspects.

The rift was made public when *The Advertiser* newspaper picked up the story about the cover and the re-launching of the anthology. The Women's Adviser to the Premier, Carol Treloar, was quoted as saying that the cover showed 'gross stupidity and incredible mismanagement'. The money problems that were bubbling away underneath would soon come to the surface, adding to the prickly relations between some Friendly Street members, but usefully drawing others together.

Unfavourable critical reaction to the Friendly Street Readers has been rare. Michael Sharkey took *No. 14 Friendly Street Reader* to task for some poetry that he felt concentrated on domestic minutiae and that displayed emotions without simplicity and intensity. At least he did note what he felt was better work. Peter Pierce, who shared his discomfort and wished to have heard the last of some of the poets, also saw work there that, 'encourages one to follow budding careers'. A mixed bag of critical responses then, but it indicates the dilemma of the editors who have to draw from the submitted material.

J M Coetzee, winner of the Nobel Prize for Literature and an Adelaide resident, was invited to select the best poem in the 2004 anthology, *Another Universe*. He commented: 'I have read the collection ... several times, with great pleasure. The general standard is high, and there are several poems that would be worthy finalists in your competition'. Poetry emerging from Friendly Street has been picked up for publication by interstate editors. Poems by Friendly Street poets have been selected by Les Murray and Dorothy Porter for their respective volumes of *Best Australian Poems*, and Bev Roberts also comments on the remarkable publishing achievements of Friendly Street, attesting to the general attractiveness of SA poetry emerging from Friendly Street.

Others, such as reviewer Noel Rowe, agree: 'Above all, (Friendly Street) is a place which not only believes poetry is alive, but which also has confidence in the power of its small press and in the collaboration which that encourages and requires'.

THE ROOT OF ALL EVIL

Money is a funny thing. We all want it but generally consider discussions of accounting matters to be dull. It seems distasteful to even mention money in the same sentence as art, but it is essential to running an organisation like Friendly Street. A succession of Friendly Street Committees has also discovered, with occasional dismay, what the planning and reporting sides of applying for state and federal funding entail.

Managing a budget that includes a publishing program is always tricky, especially with the lag between costs and eventual income. Minutes of the Friendly Street Committee attest that keeping a healthy cash flow for publishing has been a frequent problem, compounded by the fact that state and federal grants are also received late, well into the period in which they are meant to be used. Friendly Street archive notes of 1980 mention that members of the committee sometimes dipped into their own pockets to overcome a short-term gap in cash flow.

Putting together the bids for General Purpose Grants typically means setting out an optimistic, detailed range of activities that will not end up being adequately funded, and will thus have to be pruned when the actual grant is eventually announced. It chews up the Committee's time devising a program that they know will not be fully implemented but at least the exercise gets people thinking about priorities and what is most desirable. Some of those ideas may be resurrected later if more money becomes available.

The relationship between Friendly Street and its main source of external finance, Arts SA (formerly the Department for the Arts and Cultural Heritage), has been an essentially healthy one. It is our perception that, while Friendly Street could have done many more good things were additional funds made available (and what organisation in its place would not make that claim?), it has had the real support of the principal arts finding body in the state. For most of the first thirty years of Friendly Street, William Fleming and later Penelope Curtin were the key Arts SA project officers who oversaw its activities and offered advice on particular issues as they arose. Several Friendly Street Committee members have acknowledged the very valuable role that these two people have provided. Beyond their time, Alexandra Hurford and others at Arts SA have continued the tradition of working with Friendly Street. There is, after all, no other body that is more capable of representing the potential and the real achievements of poetry in this state.

Humphrey McQueen remarked at the Writers' Week launch of *Friendly St. Poetry Reader Number 6*, that 'we have to learn that government support is never neutral; it is always true that when you go to bed with the state you will get more than a good night's sleep'. Any suspicions about dealing with the bureaucracy on a regular basis must be tempered; his comment was made before the financial calamity struck in 1988. Having to account for its past activities and show effective planning for future ones has also helped to drive Friendly Street by sharpening its decision-making process. Barbara Giles, who was not connected with either Arts SA or Friendly Street, wrote that 'the generous support from [the] state government and the presence of a lively and perceptive group pledged to the art of poetry [gives] the other states ... reason for envy'. In her view then, the partnership has been a fruitful one.

Funding from the Australia Council has not always been as straightforward. It was denied to support the Readers on the basis that these were not continuing publications and, apparently, because they were anthologies – both factors placing them outside the funding guidelines. An unresolved paradox is that annual anthologies *are* often treated as continuing publication for other purposes. In 2002, a new approach was made to the Council to establish how Friendly Street might be eligible for funding to support any part of its publication program. It was decided that funding would be considered for the New Poets and Single Poet Volumes but the biggest obstacle was that this would only occur after the specific manuscripts had been selected and edited. In order to meet the Australia Council timetable, those decisions would have to be made almost a year ahead of publication, a much longer period than Friendly Street worked to. It seemed that efficiency and funding would not mix, and the publishing schedule was adjusted accordingly in order to take up the money.

The process of gathering cash at the readings was a much more interesting one in some ways than all the peregrinations within the arts bureaucracy, because it had to do with booze. Before there was such a thing as an entry fee, the interval would be when the hat would literally be passed around, a task that often fell to Rory Harris and Steve Evans (the former because it was his hat). One or both of these Friendly Street Committee members would walk to the nearby Earl of Aberdeen Hotel, carrying the proceeds. Harris remembers one hot night when he took the jingling hat there to buy wine and orange juice for the waiting poets, and found the short-staffed publican running between his three bars trying to keep up with orders. There were plenty of patrons seeking refuge in a pint that night and he was flat out dealing with everyone, while dressed only in a pair of skimpy Speedos.

These Friendly Street purchases were a known part of the alcohol culture at Friendly Street. Some poets brought their own, such as Chief Justice John Bray, who could be relied on to turn up with a flagon of wine for his fellow poets to share. Harris recalls the decision not to bother buying a liquor licence being a simple one: it was money that could be saved to spend on alcohol for the poets. Years later, there would be enough petty cash raised from charging an entry fee to allow drinks to be bought ahead of time, so they would be waiting at the venue as the night began.

Financial management of the publishing process was vested in the Friendly Street management committee. In 1986, Graham Rowlands had complained to a fellow member that the finances were beginning to be an embarrassment. Bills and royalties remained unpaid, and he applied pressure in the hope that there would be a remedy. The financial position was reasonable enough to keep things alive, but the true position was not clear and in 1988 it suddenly threatened to end Friendly Street altogether. That was when it was discovered that nearly $13,000 had gone 'missing'.

Jeri Kroll, Graham Rowlands and Rory Harris, three members of the management committee at the time, quickly denied any impropriety and, indeed, it became clear that the responsibility lay with the remaining member. It was Rowlands who sought legal advice and then undertook the complicated and delicate matter of negotiating with the various suppliers, the bank, the Department for the Arts, and the Literary Arts Board of the Australia Council. He, in particular, was deeply affected by the incident, describing the perpetrator as suffering 'some kind of illness' and being a 'pathological confidence man'.

When John Bray learned of the mismanagement details, he offered to see Friendly Street through its difficulties with a confidential loan, but this became unnecessary. It was a sign of the importance of Friendly Street for the life of poetry performance and publishing in the state (and, no doubt, also a sign of respect for Rowlands) that the South Australian Department for the Arts responded with fresh funding to enable the program to continue. In the end, no formal action was taken against the person alleged to have caused the loss, and the Friendly Street community pulled back together. The event marked a loss of innocence, however, and the organisation changed in a number of ways, mostly through adhering to conditions attached to the new funding. The publishing program became less ambitious and Friendly Street became more bureaucratic: a constitution was developed, a conventional committee was established, and regular administrative meetings were held. If there were a sense of betrayal that subtly altered the atmosphere at subsequent readings, most of the moves to a more formal conduct of Friendly Street affairs hardly registered with newcomers, who seemed to enjoy the monthly readings without giving such matters a thought.

The event was a watershed for Friendly Street, Graham Rowlands feeling this more than many. He had been a prime mover in the publishing program and much of the running of Friendly Street up to that time. Soon after the funds were embezzled, he believed that Friendly Street was 'utterly destroyed' and that the 'old guard' was too exhausted and unwilling to face the new formalities, so it would be an inexperienced new group that had to pick up the pieces. Partly out of fear that Friendly Street records could be open to the 'criminal', as Rowlands repeatedly termed the perpetrator, he placed his own and some Friendly Street materials with the Special Collections section of the library at the Australian Defence Forces Academy (part of the University of NSW in Canberra), with himself as their caretaker*.

Why is the one accountable for this crisis not named? There are several reasons. The person allegedly responsible for the loss was never charged with an offence – and who could set up a trial? Suffice to say, the identity of the supposed culprit is well known in Friendly Street circles. The person concerned has established a new life elsewhere, and Friendly Street did overcome its difficulties and move on. The incident can't be glossed over altogether but it reveals some of the problems that small arts organisations can face, especially unincorporated ones that rely on goodwill and have few effective internal controls.

Appropriate changes *were* made after the loss was

---

* The authors had Rowlands' permission to access those records for the purpose of this book, which they are pleased to acknowledge.

discovered, even if it took a while for their need to sink in. It was a significant incident that does linger in the minds of some Friendly Street regulars, as a warning not to take the continued existence of the readings and publishing program for granted.

When differences arise among Friendly Street members, they are dealt with civilly and without disruption at the readings – with one or two exceptions, anyway. Most of the little infighting that has occurred seems to have been private. Brian Forte recalls that 'at one stage, one faction within Friendly Street was known to be ringing various members of the Australia Council's Literature Board and abjuring them not to give any funds to anyone within another faction'. Given the timing of his comment, it seems most likely that this involved the split that occurred at the time of the embezzlement, but it is not corroborated.

In all, Friendly Street is fortunate that it has had strong supporters, privately and in the arts bureaucracy. Though funding to the arts has generally suffered in real terms in recent years, we should be glad at least that we have had, in Mike Rann, a State Premier who is willing to assert: 'I am particularly passionate about poetry . . . Poets play an important role in documenting and registering the emotions of our culture', and who has been willing to attend a reading at Friendly Street.

THOSE MANAGEMENT BLUES
(AND JOYS)

In the beginning, Friendly Street had a committee to organise its readings and release the anthologies. When the publishing program for works by individual poets emerged, it was run by a collective, as mentioned earlier. This group was subsumed into the general management committee that, but for the very early years, has had a membership open to annual election. The task of running Friendly Street has necessarily become more demanding of time and expertise over the years. It seems contradictory to speak of poetry and business in the same sentence but a thorough and methodical approach to the running of Friendly Street became essential; handling money and liaising with government bodies that provide much of that money tend to require it.

Committees are made up of human beings, with not only the potential for harmony and great achievements, but also for disappointment, friction and misunderstanding. In 1980, some members of the committee would address each other as the 'Gang of Four' in correspondence, a more or less comic allusion to the Chinese administration of the time, which also indicated something of the power that they wielded in Friendly Street. Graham Rowlands' patience was tried in 1983 when a committee member began to bring 'an interloper' to meetings, one who became inappropriately involved in what he regarded as crucial decision-making. As a result, he wrote a letter of resignation, but he was persuaded to withdraw it. This wasn't the end of such difficulties.

The financial loss of 1988 was a jolt for Friendly Street regulars, especially as most people would not normally have considered the importance of cash flow for the continuation of the readings and publishing activities. They would have assumed that the various Friendly Street characters they knew were working reliably in its interests, so the embezzlement was seen as a betrayal. As explained previously, the Friendly Street Committee met with Arts SA, which eventually supplied rescue funding, and the alleged culprit moved interstate. Not surprisingly, some resentment remains even now among Friendly Street regulars of that period towards the person responsible but more recent arrivals at Friendly Street are generally oblivious to the incident, as one would expect.

Newcomers to the committee can take for granted the smooth running of its events, which occur with no more than the normal level of nervousness about financial matters. The funding problem was not the only issue on the new Committee's plate after the money crisis since there were other administrative issues to deal with.

Ann Timoney Jenkin, the Friendly Street Committee Convenor in 1992, wrote in notes for a special planning meeting, that the years since 1988 had seen big changes: organising a constitution; creating regular minutes and meetings; establishing a firm working relationship with Wakefield Press for publishing and distribution of Friendly Street titles; systematically answering correspondence; restoring credentials with funding bodies; and maintenance of the standard publishing program while also ushering in new types of book. The previous committee, she claimed, had left 'in a cloud of dust, bearing with them all records and references and the keys to the mail box'. Minutes of one meeting in 1989 noted that someone had been tampering with mail in the post box, so the key was changed. While the comment about the outgoing committee seems harsh, there is no doubt it was a time of considerable adjustment.

Ralph Bleechmore remarked in his speech at the 1992 launch of Friendly Street titles in the Adelaide Festival of Arts that the publishing program of Friendly Street was 'very much a cooperative one'. He proceeded to thank a number of people including the 'Friendly Street Management Committee', which he described as 'the only one of its type left in the world following the collapse of the Soviet Union'. It was a wry comment but there was truth in its suggestion of a collective approach where the participants have backed their faith in a common cause with personal effort. This was especially the case with the first few years' publications of individual poets' books

In any case, comprehensive records were being maintained and an archive of activities and decision-making was also being developed. The availability of more detailed information has become a key ingredient in how the Committee sees its constituency. In 2001, lawyer David Adès (who had attended Friendly Street since 1979) thought Friendly Street was in the doldrums. After co-editing one of the Readers, he decided to use some of his twelve months' leave from his salaried position to work on the committee. In his time, a number of significant changes were made, including: establishing a database of Friendly Street poets and their publications; a detailed analysis of numbers attending the readings; setting up a mailing list for marketing purposes; examining the rate of first publication of poets, and much more. The fruits of these endeavours are still evident – Friendly Street now has a raft of information about who comes to its readings and who appears in its annual anthologies. This assists the committee in its decision-making and in its reports to the main funding body, Arts SA.

It may seem unfair to highlight Adès, just one person, when so many have contributed to the welfare of Friendly Street. There have certainly been many in a true community of writers who have shared the responsibility and the pleasure of keeping Friendly Street afloat. John Bray and Ralph Bleechmore, in particular, helped get Friendly Street through the legal and bureaucratic maze of incorporation in 1988. It was John Bray who quickly offered to keep Friendly Street afloat when its finances were in crisis. Ralph also asked Steve Evans to come back on board the committee as he was then a practising management accountant and had served on earlier committees in the role of Treasurer.

On a more administrative level, Betty Collins has worked for a long time to assemble records of who has appeared in each anthology, allowing an overview of such things as which poets have endured at Friendly Street. Others have laboured for no other reward but to see Friendly Street continue as a vibrant venue for poetry in Australia.

It has always been a goal, once Friendly Street stepped into the government-funding loop, to show that it could hope to eventually operate independently of such financial backing. Friendly Street is in better financial shape than ever but it is true that it still relies to a great extent on the goodwill of the State government through Arts SA, for key financial support. This says more about the typically difficult status of small arts organisations than the role they play in sustaining a vital activity in the community.

Money issues will always be complicated with the need to make a case for external financial support, and a strong, informed Friendly Street Committee is instrumental in achieving that. The records of all these issues and the various decisions that have been made help to paint a picture of Friendly Street through the years. One day some generous person (perhaps assisted by a modest grant) will collect all of the post-1988 Friendly Street papers and organise them into a more accessible filing system. Running a community poetry performance and publishing concern successfully for more than thirty years is a mighty achievement, and it would be a shame not to properly preserve the records in a manner that allows such access.

Could we look forward to the possibility that the State Library, for instance, might recognise the value of these records and offer them a suitable home? This would be a boon for lovers of poetry and other future researchers.

AFTER THIRTY YEARS

While critical of a certain romantic notion that is often attached to poetry, author Humphrey McQueen argues that Friendly Street is one instance when one should place faith in the abilities of everyday people to organise for good:

> I do not believe that poetry can change the course of history – whatever might have been the case, poets are not the unacknowledged legislators of humankind; rather, they continue to be unofficial ombudspeople for suppressed passions, personal as well as political. Poetry cannot prevent the barbarism of world war three ... nonetheless, the cooperative activism of Friendly Street is a miniature of the ways in which war and other barbarisms can be prevented, that is, by organising the strengths of working people.

This was in 1982, the year in which the Reader was launched alongside collections by five individual poets – Friendly Street in a show of force. Although McQueen was speaking more than twenty years ago, the essential sentiment of trust and cooperation within a small-group dynamic has underpinned Friendly Street since its inception. There were troubles on the horizon at that time, yes, but ones that were overcome without destructive repercussions.

A list of poets who have been prominent at Friendly Street would take more space than most readers would probably abide in a book of this kind, there have been so many. They make their impression more widely than in Friendly Street activities. A number of the poets whose interviews comprise the book edited by Ioana Petrescu and Naomi Brewer, *Heart of the Matter: An Introduction to Eighteen South Australian Poets*, for example, are or have been connected with Friendly Street. Many notable Australian poets' writing careers have been marked by an association with Friendly Street, and details can be found on the Friendly Street website.

Mike Ladd

Graham Rowlands

Geoff Goodfellow

Jan Owen

Ann Timoney Jenkin

Peter Eason

Jeri Kroll

Erica Jolly

Dave Cookson

Elaine Barker

David Adès

Jude Aquilina

Steve Evans

Louise Nicholas

David Mortimer

Rory Harris

Margaret Fensom

Barbara Preston

Nigel Day

Juan Garrido Salgado

Annette Marner

Khail Juredeini

Gail Walker

Jo Dey

Kerryn Tredrea

Ivan 'Avalanche' Rehorek

Richard Tipping

Friendly Street's original home: the Media Resource Centre in the former Gordon Sim Choon fireworks factory, Union Street, Adelaide (seen from Rundle Street East)

Friendly Street's second location: The Federal Box Factory, Regent Street, Adelaide

Friendly Street's current site: the South Australian Writers' Centre,
Malcolm Reid Building, Rundle Street East, Adelaide

Friendly Street has offered an opportunity for poets to hone their work in performance and, with luck, to see it published. Literary critics have generally been kind about the publications, but it is normal for reviewers to sometimes see anthologies as being of mixed quality. In looking back through the anthologies ourselves, we see that they were struck by how well much of the poetry endures.

Why does Friendly Street itself continue to succeed? In 1985, Carol Treloar wrote:

> It is a sign of loyalty and commitment that Friendly Street still has many of its original members and aficionados; even more, it is an exciting indication that the regular readings have taken on a rich life of their own, attracting newcomers and new blood, allowing poets from Adelaide, interstate and overseas the precious freedom to display and test their talents and to perform in a climate frequently controversial, but unfailingly sustaining in its diversity.

Adelaide poets with different tastes and styles might be said to find a respectful co-existence with each other because the city is not big enough to sustain viable readings for all of the possible splinter interests. Cornelis Vleskens wrote that 'Friendly Street ... has brought together the various divergent streams of poetry and there is no one school or ideal which is given prominence'. In 1986 poet and critic, Barbara Giles, put the continued life of Friendly Street down to 'informality, a wide umbrella, the diverse nature of its membership, the balance of age groups and sexes, its democratic structure, its avoidance of issues.' We're not so sure about the last point except if it refers to Friendly Street having no particular social or political cause to embrace. Giles also went on to say that the size of Adelaide allowed it to be 'friendly, easily accessible, manageable in size, and with a nice mix of people.' She felt that Adelaide, unlike larger cities, was not inclined to form enclaves and rivalries but, instead, to encourage cross-fertilisation.

This is obviously a common sentiment. Essayist and former Friendly Street regular, Brian Forté, also believes that part of the success of Friendly Street has been the size of the city, which is too small to support much separatism, whatever the differences between the poets. He says that people of 'various poetic ancestries ... constitute the diversity and friction which both give Friendly Street its impetus and necessitate its communal aspects'. Jeri Kroll agrees, adding that in the period from the mid 1970s to early 1980s, there was also a sense of Adelaide poets supporting each other because they felt overlooked by the eastern states. And as Jeff Doyle remarked about public reading groups in Australia, and Friendly Street in particular: 'none seems to have lasted as long, nor to have produced as much as this South Australian group'.

Not everyone has seen the success of Friendly Street as an unalloyed good. Jamie Grant qualified his view that 'the genuine friendliness of the Adelaide readings explains their long continuance', with the fear that this 'way of thinking precludes intelligent criticism' and produces a narrow dependence that he believed to have always been typical of Australian literature. Grant was reviewing two of the original collections of individual Friendly Street poets. He cited Clive James's comment that Australia's population could not sustain magazines that could afford to reject copy. In this environment, he felt, there is a lack of rigour in editing that in turn promotes weak writing. Most reviewers seem to disagree with Grant on this score, at least as far as the quality of the Friendly Street titles is concerned since they have been at least kind and often strongly approving in their public assessments. And Friendly Street has prospered since his review, with many critically received publications in that time.

A few Friendly Street characters from the early period still appear at the monthly readings to experience and help to create an evening of great poetry. They share with a great cohort of newer and younger poets the desire to maintain

Friendly Street as a vital community of writers. Friendly Street continues to be intermeshed with poetry activities on a statewide basis, and especially in Adelaide. Its writing community is big enough to expose fakes and small enough to encourage willing writers to work together for a common good. Friendly Street is still the hub for poetry in South Australia. It is a meeting place and a performance venue. It is a collective expression of support for reading and publishing poetry. Its members appear at other venues around Adelaide and interstate, and a number of them have been on the steering committees of such bodies as Poetry Unhinged, the poetry festival for the southern areas of Adelaide. Together they constitute a force for taking poetry seriously.

The 'Friendly Street Poets 30th Anniversary Reading' was held on 11th November 2005 in the State Library of South Australia. The special guest was Richard Tipping, who had helped to organise the first readings and then the first Friendly Street poetry anthology. He recalled the energetic Adelaide poetry scene in the early '70s, the visit by Allan Ginsberg and Lawrence Ferlinghetti, and the makeshift but enthusiastic nature of publishing poetry magazines before describing the genesis of Friendly Street. 'If you're willing to stand up and have a go,' he said, 'that's an act of bravery.' Tipping pointed out that the unnamed figure reading by candlelight on the cover of the first anthology was Aleks Danko. Numerous other poets then read, prefacing their work with details of Friendly Street history that were significant to them. The readings were recorded for later broadcast on radio. It started as a very civilised affair compared to the original readings at Friendly Street itself, though some irreverence and a certain amount of standing on tables eventually crept in. When it was Graham Rowlands' turn, he presented Tipping with five pristine copies of the very first anthology, to be signed and later auctioned.

According to David McCooey, despite dire prognostications for Australian poetry a decade ago, 'contemporary poetry is in the paradoxical position of both thriving and merely surviving'. If it's not reasonable to expect great wealth and recognition from poetry then Friendly Street has certainly both thrived and survived. There were times when it seemed unlikely to endure so long, yet in many respects it can be said to have done better than its counterparts, not least in longevity. The continuity of its readings and of its publishing program is testament to that. Friendly Street has had its dramas; it has confronted both the possible loss of its venue and financial difficulties. It has had colourful moments during readings, such as competing with loud Turkish music from belly dancing classes on the floor above, and fights. There have been a few dangerous liaisons in the background. There has been heckling and there has been laughter. Some important faces are no longer to be seen and many new ones have appeared. There has been a great deal of wonderful poetry and also a sense of belonging.

Andrew Taylor once remarked that the *No. Two Friendly Street Poetry Reader* was so named because it was a metaphor for a street with individual houses in it. That street is slowly developing and, if we extend the metaphor, many of its early inhabitants have grown and moved away (often to recognition on a larger stage) but still visit from time to time. There is a fresh bunch of faces in the houses at the newest end of Friendly Street and it looks growing for a long time.

Is there life for Friendly Street after 30? There sure is! To accommodate growing demand, readings start at 7:00pm and sometimes finish near midnight. A typical night of readings offers an audience of up to 100 people the chance to hear 55–60 poets strut their stuff. Another sign of the popularity of Friendly Street is that extra readings were held away from the normal venue in 2007 with forays into Salisbury and Port Noarlunga, in the northern and southern suburbs, respectively. In 2008, there is even more in store. Poets will travel to Port Augusta in the mid-north of the state for a special reading, and funding has been obtained for a regular Friendly Street program on Radio Adelaide.

If you are going to start Australia's longest running series of community poetry readings, here's a successful recipe: choose a disused fireworks factory as your venue; hold the initial reading on the day that the Governor General sacks the country's elected government; and call it Friendly Street.

A night at Friendly Street may expose the audience to some demanding material and to remarkable new work. The readings sometimes bristle with exchanges between poet and audience, even if generally more polite than they were in the first few years, and Friendly Street still burns with a passion to keep its public readings and its publication of poetry going strong. South Australia and the arts are much the better for it.

POEMS FROM THIRTY
YEARS OF
FRIENDLY STREET
ANTHOLOGIES

Adèle Kipping

TARONGA ENGAGEMENT

What passion
drives male tortoises
to join the waiting line of females?
No evidence of, May I have
the pleasure of this courting dance?
No pinched behind or questioning eyebrow.
Only that dogged unromantic process.
The males materialise
plod heavily with purpose.
No need to rush, they've more than a hundred years.
Eyes shut, she stands firm.
Never to seem too eager. Better to take
a nap while he plans his overture.
When he mounts and settles on her shell,
he stays up there trying to remember
what this is all about.
And only she could know the end result.
Couples
perpetuate the species
every spring and seasons in between;
fixed in that solid line
like idle double-decker buses
out of gas.

Aidan Coleman

FOR MY SHOWER

You make
such immaculate weather

You are a sun
before sun rise
a flower bringing rain

You colour every morning
in forgetfulness

I only ask
to hide
a moment longer
in your shining hair

No wonder so many songs
are sung to you

Allison Moore

A WORD NOT A SENTENCE

1. Diagnosis

A grey marble
like the ones we clinked in gutters
filled our pockets and went home beaming
floats in yellow liquid.

The silent killer has cast his alley
scattered my circle
collected his prize
stayed to play again.

Soft voices penetrate swirl
I connect; remember exercises
deep breaths, turn ankles
side to side, up, down,
sheets bind; I disconnect;
hallucinate in haze;
throw my dog a stick.

Doctor checks a train track of staples
talks of winning
joins my circle
leaves me to finish the game

Andrew Taylor

A MEMBER OF THE CRYSTAL SET

If the cat wants to go out
worlds we cannot deny
wait on its whiskers

and if my fingers prod the twittery dark spaces
of the radio
something that's still not speech
needs guiding in

I'll try to bring it in –
I've been caught too
by crosscurrents and undertow
and know what it means
being brought in
clear
by a cat's whisker
searching the glittering black cliffs
for a sensitive spot to come aground

Anna Brooks

EVENING CONVERSATION

stars fall from our mouths
pinpricks of light
on our lives
between so much
unspoken darkness

Avalanche

INHERITING MY FATHER'S TOOLBOX

There's a trick to opening this toolbox
first, make sure you're up the right way
because the lock may be broken, but the latch is just fine
and there's a treasure trove of memories once the lid pops
the hinges squeak and the light comes flooding in:

there's a tray of nails to hold up the stars
a puncture-repair kit for lost illusions
a sharp sharp knife for skinning nightmares
an old sepia print of Neil Armstrong by daVinci
and a pair of pliers for old regrets and wrong ideas

next, a snuff-box full of bent notes from Mozart
a tin of sardines and figs courtesy of Jonah
a whole roll of negatives from Plato
a fine old hammer to nail down arguments
and a half-jar of skin-repair, Joan of Arc brand –

So lay it all out carefully, blow off the dust and the cobwebs
(the old seals are still good and strong)
and you will need your father's tools one of these days –
first make sure you're up the right way
because there's a trick to opening this tool box.

Barry Westburg

TO MINNIE MOUSE

a red bow!
I think I'm falling
for a *mouse!*
long lashes kinkety legs
– brighter than Mickey
– always get your way
– smarter than Popeye's girl
I love you in polka dots
'fear of flying' sunglasses

black is beautiful!
you carry yourself so well
in primary colours
and you've got a lot of
scutter and pure *nous*

good for a quickie
but always a step ahead
of the big bad wolf

when Mickey's got the flu
where can I find you?

Beate Josephi

IN PRAISE OF A SECOND LANGUAGE

A second language
is like a room of one's own
to retire to at night
when the letters and phone calls have been answered
the demands for attention have ceased.

Then I can push away the still lingering phrases
and go into a clear uncluttered space of words
untouched by today. Today, for all I know
was a mere construction in another language
to be discontinued at the turn of a key.

And I turn the key and my words
are slowly coming home
homing in on the waiting
like waiting for the bus at the river
the river grey and heavily loaded with ships.

I enter the bus, go past the barracks
the chemical factories
the buildings my father spent forty-two years
of his working life in.
The cement works.

The conductor is calling the familiar names
calling up names from the past
vernacular names from the Roman past
names of the islands which hosted
tournaments and royal elections.

Until the bus goes over the bridge
and I arrive at the 'Emperor's Gate'
in another state but not another language
which I will not leave until I leave
this room of my mind.

Bridget Porter Oldale

THE REVENGE OF THE FAIRIES

*To Wm. Blake, Esq., late poet and master engraver of
London Town*

Dear Blake, I read from these lines that you caught
(and I quote) a little fairy man, and that
you straightway put him in your hat.

Lackaday. I am a little old myself for such ploys
now, and besides, worst of all, the fairies have grown
so bloody big and tall nowadays. Some of them
are fully thirty feet high,
equipped with stormy petrel wings as black
as thunderheads that block out half the sky.
Moreover they carry hand adzes and flamethrowers,
and no longer even pretend to dispense advice.

Most of them live in marshes deserts bogs forests
and mountains rather than in daisies on the lawn
or down by the potting shed at Pooh Corner.
And they do not so much swing in cowslip bells
as come thundering down the chimney hurling boulders
icebergs candlesticks teatrays besoms and old skulls all
    around the room.
I am a fairy myself through my mother
and grandmothers, the turnip and coalpit fairy,
so I speak as one who knows.

Bronwen Levy

BURIAL: EAST MAITLAND, 1981

lowering her into the ground
from the height of our shoulders
this box of polished wood
heavier than her

a paddocky cemetery, strung between industry
a sawmill, the railway line
all the flat marshes
her clear flame reaching into the wind

the black hearse bears its contradiction
a flanders field of flowers
sealed off in cellophane

the clouds halt, the grass stills, we observe
clutching at roses
the way the earth shifts
movement continuing

o jesus send her air
she is dissolving
from her joyous lips
no cry of *save me*

Christine Churches

MY MOTHER AND THE TREES

She shook the doormat free of dogs,
struck the tank to measure water, as she
marshalled us with iron buckets
to carry rations for the trees.

From fibres of air, she wove us there
the hope of leaves,
and in the flat and tepid dust
she dreamed a dwelling place of shade.

Summer by summer we carted water, slopped
lopsided up and back across the paddock:
the promised land a skeleton of stakes and hessian,
her voice insistent that they lived.

Reluctant slaves and unbelievers,
we sat out of sight
with our feet in the buckets, as she
filled the sky to the brim with trees.

Colin Thiele

MEMO: ADMINISTRATOR TO SWALLOW

Each day you come, swallow,
to my sill
to see if I sit stodgily
in my chair still.
Eyes bright and astonished
thinking it farce
that such creatures in cages
should be preserved behind glass.

Even your friends line ledges
if they can
to observe incredulously
fish-bowl man.

Then with twitters of laughter
wry and spare
follow witch-knuckle paths
on the high free air.

Swallow I admit
true, true, true,
you know more about life
than I do.

Constance Frazer

STARLINGS

Odd cloud that twists
and shapes itself

proving its strength
against the wind, suddenly reels

pours out its whole length
– a living liquid down the sky

shatters on power lines into
smithereens of squeals.

A thousand raging bird-bodies
dispute their right to an inch

of wire – who a moment since
in unison, had the whole sky!

David Adès

HAAD RIN, KO PHANGAN, THAILAND

The sea is a placid blue bowl
rimmed by white beaches and coconut palms.

I am a goldfish
eyes peering at the world, uncomprehending.

*

I rattle and throw the bones,
rattle and throw the bones.

When I lean over to decipher their meaning
they speak in a language I do not know.

*

The space I occupy follows me everywhere
like a faithful dog.

The distances I have harvested
prowl in my shadow.

*

A stranger walks upon the sand
wearing my sarong.

I catch myself in the act
of becoming someone else.

David Cookson

ASPECTS

I
As she arranges irises
to blue-shadow the room
that lock of hair falls from her temple again
its grey so silvered by sun
I could count each strand flirting with lips,
parted as if to speak.

II
She is a black paper cut-out
appliquéd on dawn
heels, pencils tapping time,
echo along a road
rain-washed to pewter.
I watch for her to glance back
face a moonstone in the leaden light
but she turns the corner, leaves my day bare.
Silence earthy with wood smoke,
irises blue flames in our tall vase.

David Mortimer

EARLY TRAIN TO TOWN

There's a woman dreaming at the end of the carriage
Eyes shut and a smile
Riding like an angel against the people in the next carriage
With one glass triptych behind
Another sometimes framed, sometimes hurled

Left or right, above below across
The lurch of uncertainty distance
The chain-swung swivelled between
Nervous half-curving held-apart
Bounce and recovery, limbo of coupling, uncoupling
A sudden card-board cut-out saint, deity, the Buddha
A magnetic chess piece interposed, photograph unstuck
Unglued and ouija'd across a scrapbook
Beatifically swirled

Against an unconcern of newspapers
Schoolbags, coats, faces pressed to background
Hands gripping, swinging handles
She is in the eternal
Present world, whirled inward
An index case of calmness, finger of God
Eyes shut and seeing the eternal
Living suburbs passing in a true city
Open in another world

Deb Matthews

THE SWING

The swing is a musical instrument.
The sound of a badly played violin
when bow grates across strings.
It sings rhythm and rust.
A violin with many seats and room for standing.
It draws the shrieks of children's voices
through the blue score of the sky.
It is a concert of discords
with its creaks and screams
that counterpoint the tune –
but always the
    rhy – thm
        rhy – thm
            rhy – thm

Deborah McCulloch

THINGS A MAN MAY DO

play in a band
plant trees
look at the stars
drawing maps is a little too close
and healing should never be allowed
waiting on tables
training horses
building some things
but keep them away from words
cleaning the streets is OK
dredging channels or swimming pools
building railways is too permanent

it's a pity
they're so bad at serving
of course they've never been
properly taught
if they could take 'Put it down there, boy,'
a little easier, there'd be no
trouble at all.

And yet entertainment is
so powerful; nature is what they're
closest to and should be kept for,
their muscles are adapted to it,
it's obvious. Such restless
demanding creatures,
never satisfied with what they've got.
There'll be rebellion there, mark my words;
a generation is all it will take
unless we're firm this time,
now.

Deborah Thomas

THE GORGE

The children asked me to tell them
About the Columbia Gorge.
A woman once threw her babies into it.
That was all they wanted to know.
I drew a blackboard diagram for them,
Of two projectiles falling,
White dashes behind to show the speed
At which they drew near the river.
I brought in Galileo's study, mentioning
In passing, Northwest fossils,
The particularly interesting strata
The children had passed by,
All the natural bridges in the vicinity
From which they did not fall.

The children wanted to know
If I had been there to see it
Where she dumped the babies
From the suspension bridge.
My car had stopped there once,
For a moment, and I recognised her urge.
I wondered if juries took field trips.

Where the white specks whizzed
Past layer upon layer of explanation,
Where the chalk bones blended
With those of ancient fish
I drew an Indian
White with dust
And fear of falling stars.

Diane Fahey

ANDROMEDA

She was the first pin-up.
Naked and bejewelled,
she was chained to a rock,
then thrown by heavy-breathing
winds into wild postures:
at each new angle, lightning
popped like a photographer's flash.

The gold circling her neck
matched her hair, the emeralds
her eyes, the rubies her nipples,
and the amethysts those bruises
covering her skin, once pearl-
white as for all princesses.

In lulls of wind, she pulled
against iron, stood almost straight.
The sky was a mouth swallowing her,
the sun a glimmering eye;
lolling in the tide, a sea-dragon
slithered and gargled like
some vast collective slob.

From afar, Perseus saw her first
as a creature writhing on a rock;
close up, she was a whirlpool
of rage and terror and shame.
The dragon he changed to stone
with hardly a thought. But
his strength almost failed him
in breaking those chains.

Looking away from her nakedness,
he smooths her ankles, wrists.
She waits for the moment
when he will meet her eyes.

Donna McSkimming

BEDROCK

I buy apple cucumbers because of you
the wet weight and slight prickle
that you grew   I remember the genus
of birds   your love shown by explaining
small things   I excavate layers of memory
for you   a white towelling hat
slightly grubby   long socks and spit
polished shoes   your medals
clothes bought by your wife
the long years sold to duty   the rages
at my mother   the unintelligible writing
I must sift   till the words are revealed
my mother could translate that script to five children
but what is the core of this   a man
who would not lie to the court to spare his friends
who tried to lose his daughter her first job
rather than say his grief at her leaving
what bedrock you covered with your gladioli and asters
the tree you set at each new house
knowing you would never see it tall
this archaeology turns seed for fruit and flowers
and a stem of backbone golden wattle flaunting
in the smog of Newcastle   a cupped hand
and my penchant for naming   something written
and indelible   though not understood
amid a rubble of affection

Elaine Barker

SHADES

(at the Holocaust Museum, Washington, DC)

If it were not for the fact
that the fabric was missing,
rotted right away, you'd imagine
this clutch of umbrellas had been readied
for the proverbial rainy day.
But only the metal skeletons remain,
seared, angular, stacked together,
smelling of rust and flame.
Recalled forever from alleyways,
paths, lanes, streets, roads,
from linden-lined boulevards,
these frames have outlived their ends.
So you can only guess at the hands
that would have grasped them
under screaming skies,
against the wind and the rain
and the crumpled stars.

Eric Beach

I HATE POETRY

I hate poetry
   those readings where you sit still
               until th chairs ache
& you stare fixedly at th wax flies on th ceiling
& someone's great thoughts
               roll around in heads untenanted
like city buildings on empty nights
               & th lonely words
                  window-shopping
I hate poetry
   I hate butterflies
          I hate electric shock
I hate someone putting a thrill thru me
               romantic poems as painful
as th one you love calling long distance
               I like massed one-man bands
I want poetry to be a little nervous about opening th door but only
because it's in a hurry to get to th bed I've never been to bed with a poem
               most poems would be too stuck up
for hundreds of years
poetry vanished
     into th blankness
          between th legs of dolls
suddenly
    poetry discovered that it had pubic hair
               & beneath the hair
a crude sketch of genitalia
         meet me here at 3 o'clock
               act suspicious
poetry that never turned up
         poetry that played cruel jokes

a rose painted black & laid on a young girl's pillow
poetry that's always pressing
                              in like earth
                                             always on about graves
I'd rather fill in
                th gaps between friends
I hate poetry
                I won't be caught, like cassius
                                             dead with poetry
poetry is a train of thought that refuses to arrive

Erica Jolly

PAPERBARK
(Thinking of Oodgeroo Noonuccal)

While sun-lit blossoms
summon all in season

and suede-like peeling bark
speaks more than parchment,

sinuous roots slowly
reveal their strength,

snake through
suburban drains,

crack ceramic pipes
                              and legal fictions.

Flexmore Hudson

BASHŌ

Bashō, the ragged poet, the wanderer Bashō,
astride a sleepy horse at the edge of a rustling pond
where teal, at the splash of a salmon, sail for clumps of bamboo.

High on the opposite bank, a gusty pine is waving
across the noon-white snow of distant Fujisan,
pouring cascades of gold-dust, luminous, gentle as mist,
on blue sky, blue ripples, and morning glory bells.

And his horse is drowsing, drowsing – a dragonfly close to its ears! –
while Bashō, brushing the gold from its glossy mane, is smiling
that such a little thing as pollen clouding a wind
should outweigh the fifty sorrows, the disillusioned years.

G M Walker

LIFE

an illusion
I reinvent
every morning

Gaetano Aiello

OPENING AN UMBRELLA

I grasp the handle
of my umbrella
I sense the stirring
of the nocturnal,
the wings of a giant fruit bat
wriggle; grey flaps dangle
cartilage struts straighten
and skin tightens around the
frame of my shadow
as I walk down Grenfell Street
into the night.

Geoff Kemp

THE WAR VETERAN'S PRAYER

The gunfire is somewhere else now.
Rusted chassis and tripods,
shell cases, buried bones,
the thud of artillery, screaming men,
bullets zinging the grass
      all covered now
           by wet growth
           or packed-down walking trails

Men walked out of here, young
but forever cut-off
           from the certainties they were defending.
Our letters, photos,
dream-glimpses of a woman, child, mother,
backyard swing or fishing spot

have become whatever the future is,
their obliteration
           a music in the rustling grass
              if you're prepared to listen ...

Will the vigour of my son's spirit
bursting over the edge of the unknowable
run at smacking bullets
or holler laughter
           at something better than war?

I pray that he'll lie, in long grass,
dripped on by fat leaves,
with one ear to the ground,
the other to the eternal reassurance
we call mystery,
his arm holding a girl,
           or the hope of one,
with no emptiness in his heart.

Graham Catt

THE HIERONYMUS BOSCH SHOPPING MALL

the mall is decorated with bones
the mall is decorated with bats and ants

the security guards have pitchforks and horns

there are goats and birds and beetles in the mall
there is a lizard playing a harp made of human limbs
there is a girl cutting her hair with a fish

there are crowds of naked people
they climb an escalator of fire
they are beaten by winged monkeys

in the food court
        a priest is being eaten by a mandolin
        a hag slices virgins into a frying pan
        a vending machine dispenses worms

the shops sell knives and rats and brooms

the checkout operator is a giant owl
the store manager has a pig on her head
the trolleys have teeth and scales and claws

there is a carpark for sinners, and a carpark for saints

      the carpark for sinners is full

Graham Rowlands

THE DAFFODILS

They're not lemon or golden or almost orange, they're
a potion of dye yellow, these unwrapped daffodils
frilling from their most open buds, antique,
their inner cylinders empty, economical.

The same bulbs sprouting in the same place.
In the time & space of one year's turning
again they're all here, bending towards me.
Jacarandas filter light. The brushfence saws off
the sun & they bend south for the other Tropic, straining.

Last year they were shaggy brown wrappings
before I fixed my trance on the fear of red:
bags, vans, biros, fire-extinguishers, anything red.
Even Mars. I ran from nothing. Very extreme.
But stems always opened yellow –
never into dreaming's jets of blood.

After weeks into months of hiding under bedclothes
I open my door onto winter morning's dew.
Everything basks in sunbeams from a sun
like rays on a child's easel, pure yellow.
I should go down on my knees, take off my clothes,
pray to bulb & stem & daffodil & would if
I'd lapped the dew & eaten every petal.

Not that I'm not grateful for daffodils & things:
a floor, a roof, a bed, four fireplaces, windows & doorways,
daily walking to & from butcher, fruiterer, supermarket.
The impossibility of sleeping twenty-four hours a day &
of my life going on without me or me without my life.
Piss, shift, thirst, hunger & dusting day & night.

A social worker. A psychiatrist & his biology & mine
from his arsenal & battery of anti-highs & lows
modulating sodium in & outside my braincells.
No driving. No drinking. Good. A dry mouth. Bugger.

A few friends. Two cats for my wife. My wife
& the dozens of daffodils & I nod our heads & agree
that, by our time, seventy years are many.
Love works a love-change in me at last
as her lips to a daffodil meet mine to a daffodil.

If you can see the sky from where you are &
if it's not sunrise or sunset or a rainy day
what you always see every time you look up
is some shade of blue or the memory of. Now
hold up against this blue, this yellow's daffodil.

Heather Johnstone

ARRIVAL OF A 75 PER CENTER
TO THE BURNS UNIT

They wheeled him in
just before the dinner trolley
wrapped like Lazarus,
but howling
howling
so you'd know he was alive.

Heather Sladdin

THE WHITE STALLION

a rusty field
in the shadow of cloud
and one white stallion
his mane teased upwards
by electricity and the wind
galloping

rearing up
on hind legs
his hooves scratch
at the horizon
trying to enter
the invisible

Ian Reid

BEING DRAWN

Most quick to draw, she pulls
each particle of you into her pattern
like iron filings into a curvilinear field.
And that could be enough, except
that the lines arch only to and from herself.

Or to have a pencil shape you:
she puts you right in the composition,
taking the sag away from your shoulders.
But still the strong lines come from her hand alone.

Or, slowest of all, so slow, she lifts you up
from a deep green well by the rope you once gave her.
She draws you out. You draw yourself up straight.

J L Malone

VISITOR

There's something in the house.
Maybe a cat.
Maybe the wind
shouldering its way down the passage.
I open the door.
All is silent. Still.
What is it, my wife asks.
Nothing, I say, nothing.
Time passes.
A bird chortles.
Already it is dawn.
I settle down.
Soft.
There it is again,
a shuffle
a duet of whispers.
This time I leap
fling the door open
it is a girl
coming from my son's room
in stockinged feet,
her hair awash with light.
She looks at me startled
and I at her.
I walk back into the room
pretending I have seen nothing.
My son feigns sleep.
He is just sixteen.
Already it is much later than I think.

James Bradley

from PAPER NAUTILUS

I
The bones of the wrist are
delicate
        as marine origami.

Tonight
        let us talk
of Izanagi
        who
tiring of poetry
made all the world of paper.

Jan Owen

PICNIC

Blackberry season, she crammed the old black Ford
with buckets, billies, pans, Papa, and us,
passed other pickers to her secret place,
furthest, densest, deepest. Papa sighed.

The drupelet clusters glistened, witches' jewels;
her dark eyes glittered at the offering, black
blood fruit too fiercely sweet to slake,
sharp as the clawing leaves or her stained nails

that pounced and pecked, sharp as her voice
said 'Dreckly!' (then forgot) or 'Just a scratch!'
John hid and Papa tinkered with the clutch
while we picked on. The purple juice

spread over all the hills as we chugged home,
and she was Nan again, and hugged us warm.

Jeff Guess

LIVING IN THE SHADE OF NOTHING SOLID

To the old house at the end of the street
with more history in its walls than bricks:
not every year, but most, the bees would come back.
Only a few at first, to the small study-room
at the end of the long passage
and bump against the glass.
It was always at the same time; probably same day
although we never checked.
And occasionally if the window was left ajar –
before the late spring swung to summer
they would come in, and swarm on walls; furniture;
anything – looking for a hive.
And each time someone would come with boxes,
gadgets and gear and take them away.
but this year it was an old man
who walked with two sticks and didn't speak much
who brought nothing.
Asked to be shut in with them alone,
and listen to their song. Half an hour later,
he told us if we didn't want them back,
they'd have to be destroyed.
'Bees have the longest recall – and the best,
they keep coming back here – looking for their tree.'
Cut down probably a hundred years ago, but
roots still deep in their collective conscious dance;
buzzed messages of shape, type and height;
the inherited mind-maps of memory.
He poisoned the swarm and they have not returned.
And with them, the tree we never knew was there –

that died the same day,
we stopped the bees believing in it.

Jenny Boult

CUT UP/CENTURY HOTEL

i had a head injury
but i'm all right now

now that you've left me
i'm living with the possibility

that i'm an acid casualty
almost unable to cry

i wish i could advise you
about this mess of false attractions

i wander through this aural blur
wondering if it's worth listening

to so much loud noise
boys who use guitars as toys

tried so hard to write these dreams
instead i wrote a letter

about the way you used to be
think soft of you instead of reason

scream   scream
along the silence

that the universe has come to mean

Jeri Kroll

MAMMOGRAM

She no longer turns sideways to the mirror,
avoids profiles in shop windows,
anything that reflects:
car doors, washing machines,
a man's eyes as she undresses.
She puts on a bra gingerly,
as if her breasts need to be cradled
like a baby's head.

The day is a minefield of symbols.
Anything could explode.
Her children forget to kiss her goodbye,
the car stalls on the way to work,
a freak wind almost absconds
with the client's letter she reads by a window.

Finally, the present begins again.
She looks, not at reflections,
but at pale, unknowing skin.
She passes the breast over
to the radiographer,
a gift she'd rather keep for herself.

The other woman arranges it on a plate
with the tact of those who know
exactly what to write on sympathy cards.
At least she is honest –
it can hurt, she says –
as she flattens the breast
like a butterfly under glass.

The radiographer leaves to protect herself,
but the specimen's trapped.
The bruise in her mind starts to spread
even before the vessels react.
A machine hums. She imagines the picture –
a negative of lunar landscapes.

It's over quickly as promised.
She waits in a cubicle
slightly bigger than a confessional,
wondering what to repent of first – if needed.
Telling herself, it's only a scare.
Guessing at the possible cures.
The breasts, back in their cups,
tamed and sensible in cotton,
giving nothing away of the past
or the future.

Jim Puckridge

NIGHT FISHING

A boy, I rode nightly
The town jetty's bow,
Heading its long hull
into the dark,
The waves passing on starlit paths
Murmuring around the piles
In known voices, unknown tongues.

My line felt tides,
Crabs tinkering,
Nudges of bodies passing,
Or something reaching up the line
To grab, tug and drag me down
Into its underworld –
Then snap the line and leave me
Dangling and dry.

Nights I steered
Port Lincoln jetty
Into new seas,
My line sounding deeps and shoals,
Fashioning at my finger's ends
Monsters and miracles.

Jo Dey

CITY, EAST END

9.15am

In the winter sun the streetscape is
hard-edged, warmth illusory.
The man in faded green
and the dog, tousled yellow,
walk. An old dog,
once of many tricks.
It is unclear who
is walking whom.
Here, one might 'turn a few tricks',
but not in this full-cold illumination,
and intention is something that
dog and man have left aside.

10am

At 10am they appear, he white-haired
brown-skinned (holidays north perhaps),
she, dark hair pulled back with bow,
a girl, at fifty paces anyway; semblance
of fashion, apartment dwellers.
Their dog a whippet, stripped
down like any company.
Bred to shiver on marbled floors
of elevation, the low-
allergy, low-maintenance
no-bark, almost
no-dog, dog, on a short lead.
It sniffs for the scent
of its heritage along
the café-cluttered pavement.

John Bray

THE PERSIMMONS

Six tawny globes, crowned with black polar stars,
Burn on the bowl: their taut translucent skin
Rather promotes than veils what lies within,`
Like Vulcan's net when Venus tangled Mars.
Now prove these promised joys. Taste one and try.
What scraping bitterness, what clawed acridity,
What griping, green, unseasoned, thin acidity,
The palate ploughed, the puckered lip awry.
But wait: wait till the crackled stars turn brown,
The slackened skins in sagging scrollwork creep,
Or stickily in oozy patches weep.
Then boldly bite. The luscious flesh glides down.
So those to whom fair-seeming youth proves sour
In shrivelled age may see their sweetness flower.

John Griffin

OUT THERE

Last night, lugged from the deepest gully
overgrown with tangled sleep, I woke
and stumbled to the phone. It rang and rang
and rang, it seemed an hour
while I negotiated our familiar rooms.
Whoever it was, out there, breathed once,
and then hung up. The end of sleep
at half past two. Wife and children
undisturbed in the warm safe cave,
and I, twitchily awake and wanting sleep,
alert now to discern whatever menace
breathed out in the brush, or slid
under the gully's twisted shroud.
I kept the cave mouth until morning came.

Jude Aquilina

SULTRY

The street breathes into my sleep-out
huffs heat through fly screens.
The pale starless sky
is a backdrop for barking dogs.
An orange street light
inflames a row of garbage bins.

A V-8 engine throbs along the highway
and I imagine an orange Monaro
clinging like a fly to a strip of tar,
trying to escape.
Yesterday, by the petrol station
I saw a bronze girl hitchhiking,
dusty as an unearthed statue;
poised arm, tapered thumb
and singlet arm-holes stretched
enough to see a dangerous curve.

Embalmed in sheets and sweat
I drift and toss and dream
of her long plaited hair
burning in the sunset.
Airbrakes squeal,
a round of dogs fires up.
I hitch myself to daybreak.

Judy Dally

MY MOTHER DREAMS

My mother dreams she's making cups of tea
for people she doesn't know
        or doesn't like
        or doesn't want to disappoint

With tea bags that break
        or split
        or fall off their strings

In cups that overflow
        or leak
        or fall to pieces

My mother dreams she's making cups of tea
but can't find the tea
        or the cups
        or even the people she's trying to make it for

In her dreams
my mother thinks she'll die
if the tea doesn't get made

I'm afraid
she'll die
when it does.

Jules Leigh Koch

ENDINGS

At the
end of
the longest
staircase
of
stars
there will be
mornings
when
our hearts are
small birds
with clipped wings
and each truth
we keep
is a vase without
a single flower
and our hands
are idle paper
yachts
on an ocean of skin

Kate Deller

THE END OF THE DROUGHT

brought more rain
than you'd imagine

listening in the night
you smell the very hour
the tin roof stills

upon waking
in the early light
you're not surprised
at its leadenness

wet sheets strung low
tank's first overflow

or when coming down
the mountain track
that passes as a road
littered with new rockfall
branches like chewed twigs
flanked by creeks
running faster on the dirt
than you dare drive

onto the valley floor
at the view to the west
of placid cattle grazing
water lapping around their legs

and the farmer in her paddock
rubber boots kicking high
sloshing in the new green.

Kate Llewellyn

HELEN

In the middle of the Trojan war
Paris gets the hots again for Helen
he's whisked off in the midst of battle
by Aphrodite to do the deed
but Helen tells him off in no uncertain manner
and he replies 'Never has such desire overwhelmed me
not even in the beginning when I carried you off
and we spent the night on the isle of Cranae
in each other's arms . . .'
admit it
some men's timing is exquisite
the nations are at each other's throats
with spears and swords and stones
and Paris wants to lie with Helen
poor woman what was she to do
'Might as well be hung for a sheep . . .'
thinks Helen
so she did what we all have done
lay down and gave herself to love
and knew she'd pay and pay

Kerryn Tredrea

RUNNING WITH KNIVES ON A SLIPPERY SURFACE

insanity doesn't run in my family,
he walks slowly, and carries a big stick.

he takes me to the park of familiar noises and
spins me too fast on the merry-go-round.
he takes me walking through minefields in clown shoes
with my little red wagon, collecting victims and empties
and things that go thump in the night.
he takes me stalking the corners of a lifestyle that
no amount of pretending and latex will ever let me join in.
he takes me running with knives on a slippery surface.
he takes me.

he leaves me wrapped up in costumes, too afraid
to get naked.
he leaves me blessed with a vicious beauty, making
me feel more manatee than mermaid.
he leaves me confusing my muse with an addictive personality,
spitting distance from reality but it's all done
with smoke and mirrors.
he leaves me seeing my fears in double vision.
he leaves me.

he drags me along in the hand of illusion, ovld hands
for good or evil.
he drags me (kicking and screaming) down the aisle
to my permanent pew in the chapel of unrequited love.
he drags me to the roof and makes me dizzy.
he drags me under the riptide, where it's darker than
a month of new moon midnites, not waving, not drowning,
not even really treading water.
he drags me under.

insanity doesn't run.

Kevin Roberts

CIVIL RIGHTS

The Burmese lies, indigent by the stove door
stretched in the warmest spot, refuses
to move, yowls, as I shove it to put
another log in the fire, a bitter plaint
hard done by, this cat, having never caught
a single meal, except out of tins, meows,
as if anything less than temple guard
is beneath it, and it's doing us a favour
merely by living here, and suddenly
I'm annoyed at its domestic presumption,
feline acceptance of some law that says
I provide all, cut wood, stacked and
brought in obeisance to this useless fur

so I boot the damn cat, a good one,
lift it two feet and it screams off
yowling brutality to my family, each
in turn, agonised abrogation of its right

and they form a solid phalanx of reprisal,
reproach, justice, bring the bloody cat back
stroke its hurt but purring ego, place it
right in the way again, with warnings
and I know lilies in the field have
more rights than I, in this Eden,
and the damned Burmese turns, gives me
one snotty look, stretches
to luxuriate, again, by the stove.

Les A Murray

MIDSUMMER ICE
from Three poems in memory of my mother,
Miriam Murray Nee Arnall

Born 23.5.1915, died 19.4.1951
Remember how I used
to carry ice in from the road
for the ice chest, half running,
the white rectangle clamped in bare hands
the only utter cold
in all those summer paddocks?

How, swaying, I'd hurry it inside
en bloc and watering, with the butter
and the wrapped bread precarious on top of it?
'Poor Leslie,' you would say,
'your hands are cold as charity –'
You made me take the barrow
but uphill it was heavy.
We'd no tongs, and a bag
would have soaked and bumped, off balance.
I loved to eat the ice,
chip it out with the butcher knife's grey steel.
It stopped good things rotting
and it had a strange comb at its heart,
a splintered horizon rife with zero pearls.

But you don't remember.
A doorstep of numbed creek water the colour of tears
but you don't remember.
I will have to die before you remember.

Lidija Šimkuté

HUNGER PROWLS THE GRASS

The sky is pale
Clouds bony and lean
Winter eats the sun
                from my palm

The wind hides
Unbreathing
In the valley

Louise Crisp

THE MAN NEXT DOOR

The man next door is on a chain.
constantly he roams the small backyard
one bare tree he tore the leaves off
for winter
stunted garden plants trapped in the packed ground
he pokes them incessantly
prowling either side of the house
he appears any time, all the time
next door in his yard
the low tin fence cuts off his head
I've known him throat up
for months
over coffee

occasionally he goes out
on the hard stone path to the shop
bent and thin in the ugly suburb
he returns hurriedly

often the grown children visit
voices
lumps of concern, huge in his yard
photoslgn
he evades them
continues his track/up and down
the geraniums suffer him again
frustrated
they refuse ever to flower.

Louise Nicholas

THE PHOTOGRAPH

Just beyond the deferential dip of his head,
the first floundering on the thin ice of her eyes,
just out of sight, around the corner, to the left, to the right,
of the blur that is her hand reaching out to his,
a gene pool is waiting to gather.

And if you hold your breath long enough,
if you become the salted wound
between one cry of a gull's heart and the next,
if you hold a magnifying glass between the sun,
as symbol of millennia past and future
and this involuntary blink of an eye before you now,
there'll be in this image,
in the pinpoint of light before the flame,
the slow process of our becoming:

my mother, myself, my daughter, her daughter, her daughter's
daughter.
All of us and more,
teetering on the starboard of the Manly Ferry
at the precise moment of their meeting.

Margaret Galbreath

NIGHT TRAINS

The sound of a train in the night
dumps me into childhood,
shifting dunes of flock mattress
under the sloped ceiling of granny's
back room like the inside of a hill.
Night has snuffed grandad's red lamps
of apple and gooseberry, white
Star of Bethlehem, his chickens
feather-bedded dream of worms.
Even the stink of Steadman's pig
slumps on its own side of the wall.
The world's a black page for fear to write on.
Ghosts in the curtained alcove
stir between elderly coats, alive perhaps.
Something pecks at the window.
And a train like friendly cavalry
blows its far horn, gallops iron-footed
along its bank, hurls volleys of light.
Ghosts shrivel. The plum tree's
pecking fingers shine with leaves.

Maureen Vale

SERGEI KRIKALEV PONDERS
TEN MONTHS IN SPACE

In there, up there
it was too different.
Quiet, even with the crackling
radio communication.
Weightless, that ultimate floating
unlike anything they simulate.
A miniature world –
ship in a bottle
garden in a jar.
Contained absolutely
having your own existence
spinning in your own orbit.
Of course my life changed
while I took time out.
But change is measured in seconds
first grey hair
another speck of dust on a worn wall.
They kept it waiting for me, that's all.
Their capsule of time
to exchange for mine.
When they took me from the cocoon I'd spun
they wanted me be grateful.
I was thin, they said,
but they were grotesque,
cowed by gravity, pulled out of shape.
It wasn't coming back to a different place.
Not returning.
Not a homecoming.
More like a terrible birth.

Mick Bocchino

LESSON

sometime near the end of the lesson
i ask her lightly
    'where exactly are you, then?'
she smiles thinly, says –
    'oh, not here.'
we both know it's tough
to not think about the Accident.

at 14 she's old, is part and whole of this tragic ripple
that starts with the finality of death –
cars bloodwrack blood toofast now pooled
useless like mum&dad and Brad forever –
now just the pain of memory and forgetting.

minutes become lunchtime
when bells – knee – jerk – room – explodes
all soft words
but she stops,
turns,
looks our the window, says –
    'i just don't want to think anymore, ever'.

we have been taught too well
how not to share the knowledge
that we weren't so immortal after all.

Mike Ladd

POEM FOR 2 BRICKIES

Iambic below,
from stack to flick –
soft strong/soft strong/soft strong.

The mirrored trochee stands above,
strong soft/strong soft/strong soft –
catch to second stack.

Between the two,
the material
made weightless –
caesurae of an afternoon.

From clothbound hand
to clothbound hand –
each earth-fired book
placed to wait
on its invisible shelf of air.

Miriel Lenore

GENESIS

We sent the men out to the hunt today.
It was getting impossible in the cave –
we couldn't get on with our work,
couldn't get near the fire to cook.
It's alright in the summer, they potter about,
carving sometimes, dancing sometimes,
making up little rituals for the Goddess,
but when it rains . . .
So i had this brilliant idea,
i drew a large bison on the wall and said,
i think the Goddess wanted one of these.
But the men didn't go.
Lilith said, i'll sing in praise of hunting.
The men sat on.
Mela said, i'll paint you with your catch.
Still they hesitated.
Ana said, whoever brings back the bison
can sleep with the Goddess tonight.

It was so peaceful working in the cave today.
As for tomorrow . . .

Miroslav Holub

WHILE FLEEING

It was Rembrandt
or Poincaré,
or Einstein,
or Khatchaturian,
two years old,
and his mother
was shot
or buried
in rubble
while fleeing
and she was pressing him
to her breast
when she fell,
he was smothered,
and disappeared without having appeared.

When we find
small white stones
or a yellow pebble,
we play with them,
we put them together
in little piles,
letters,
and circles.

It may be an
unconscious
burial rite
for times when
there aren't any
passage graves,
cremation sites,
bronze clasps

when only
a couple of million
mothers flee
constantly flee
from somewhere
to somewhere
else.

Translated by Dana Hábová and David Young

Moya Costello

CARDIES

for Jenny Pausacker

Did Australopithecus wear them? Did we really have to wait for *Homo sapiens*, Lord Cardigan? For fundamentally, cardigans are so democratic. We wouldn't wear anything else. It's best to describe them through their opposites, jumpers. Which are too much. Jumpers are good in mountains and cardigans wouldn't go there. But cardigans do whatever cardigans do, perfectly. Cardigan is the uncommon use of the word comfortable. (Most understand slippers.) Even without pockets, cardigans are more than O.K. I particularly understand both cardigans and jumpers in red. (If we had no food, would we then not think about cardigans). Unlike naive woollen gloves, cardigans are knowing. Their purpose is not to be attractive to others. Though participating in a twin-set, they can present a kind of elegance. The ones we bought in op. shops, just arm length and flattening our chests, made us look like waifs. The ridiculous pink angora fluffies of the fifties never suited me. An aberration I thought, an abuse of their essentially practical nature. Sublime in their temperature control: open for the circulation of air, or wrapped around our bones. The girl who always wore the white one to Sunday mass. My sisters and I scorned her for it, though she didn't know. When really, she had the right idea. The way cardigans, especially long ones, go well with single women. That's why we wear them deliberately. We think of literary women (the twenties and thirties) – Virginia and Vita. Even if the cardigan was the suit coat made in cardigan style. Edith in Hotel du Lac, and she wanted to look like Woolf. Gertrude must have worn one. And Alice B. Toklas. Even Sylvia would have worn a fifties cardigan – short to the waist with pearled buttons. We wore hand-knits as children. The only thing I've ever knitted is a cardigan. In winter, candies are the most comfortable woollies around the house. I've dreamt of evening cardigans – those with beading from Hong Kong. I've come very close to owning one of these. Cardigans don't try to please anyone but us. They're a second skin. Cardigans remind us of ourselves.

Murray Bramwell

FOXFIRE

The night air is clear
small noises   intermediaries
between the black sky
and where I stand

(the hoses have been checked
the sprinklers moved
the drake with two new mates
secure within the wire enclosure
safe from foxes for a while.
The hens shuffle at their roosts
black feathers ruffling as they doze.
Cats, unsleeping, lurk and watch)

The night is mostly quiet
as I look about
cars solid and still
toys and shoes strewn under the apple tree

the pine behind the house
stands high
tall as the world
ladder for the unlit heart.

neil paech

JOHN BRAY, POET

at 77 he stands there like the fag end of a rag
a washed out specimen on a hook
bone shoulders and red gutted face
a projecting belly and trousers falling from his hips in disarray
like wasted lips off no tomorrow.
the idea of the bag is definitely in
and someone is giving a dedication to him at the podium
the crowd crowding in on them in a semi-reverent semi-circle
he the strawberries oysters and fr. champagne
of their attention. but his mind is indifferent
his eyes spiralling off on the back of a black and white magpie

out for a stroll on the lawn between them. neutral ground.
a somewhat bedraggled and intent bird
arrogant with that longlegged strut and shuffle
that produces the magic of the worm in the end
from the hat of the ground
picking it up and prodding at it
thrusting at it with vicious jerks and severs
until it disappears down the plughole of that one last time.
a worm is the ultimate in dedications
and a bird has the last word

Patricia Irvine

AFTER LES MURRAY

Loose cannon, iron balls rolling and clashing
on the tilty timber deck that was Taree treelife once,
hitting our bulwark's buffer with its shone shot,
hundreds and thousands, nonpareil, flashing
words blown out the barrel. Fire and recoil,
lithe, supple mind, truculent, trucker-capped,
blasting aspirationals and the politically correct.
Sag-shorted arse and legs, barefoot paraclete,
blessing rural rednecks, damning the elite.

You write creek-cluck and gobble, bottle glottal
netted by pen and keystroke, griddled troutlike, tagged and freed,
though sandwiched between covers for urbanites to read –
blady-grass and cow-steam, udder-shapes, mist unfurled,
psalm-sung by unkilted Scots in an ironbark Bunyah world.

Peter Eason

AUTISM OR MYSTICISM

I hit a telephone pole
And it rang hack
Standing in a paddock
Hitting a pole with a stick
It rang back
Standing and listening
To the instant
And sharp echo crack
Of a pole and stick
I stand back
Watch the swinging
Hear something else
In the sharp echo crack
For I have struck so long
The bell of Being
That I hear echoing
A silent ringing
Of my becoming
From no beginning
And I swing forward
As 1 swing back

Peter Goldsworthy

JOKES

Don't tell me jokes:
I know about jokes.
They think they are so funny.
They think they can get away with anything.

I don't know everything about them,
just enough. I know this:
that they refuse to be remembered,

slipping through the mind's fingers,
a shoal of laughter, vanishing.

And this: that they hide still inside,
deeply. Delinquent poems, absconders
from custody, safe in a safe house.

I suppose they think it a great lark
sneaking back again and again:
the grenade of laughter,
then silence.
I prefer to find it tiresome.
And a little sad.
All that repetition!

Don't pigeonhole me:
I appreciate a good joke.
I said appreciate, not laugh at.
For I will no longer laugh.
I will not answer their ridiculous summons.

I refuse to accept their subpoena.
Never again will I eagerly rip open
the scented envelope
filled with strange plastic.

There are only three jokes anyway:
the custard pie, the breaking of taboo,
the thing we are each
most afraid of.

Peter McFarlane

LULLABY
for Alexander

Adolescence half covers you
like a quilt in hot weather.
Sleep is more a recuperation
from the battle of days, where loss
is constant and you have to shout
to be noticed. You act without knowing,
wagging school, stealing from shops and
answering police and parent questions
as if you've been hit and burnt by lightning.
I want to press lullabies like hot towels
on the confusion of your loss,
or sisters leaving home and parents
in different houses. I want
to wrap up friends and put them
in pillow cases at the end of your bed,
like Christmas presents that won't fade or break
when you play with them in the morning.
Hush a bye, don't you cry.
Go to sleep my baby.

Peter Porter

THE KING OF THE CATS IS DEAD

The light on his thigh was like
a waterfall in Iceland, and his hair
was the tidal rip between two rocks,
his claws retracted sat in softness
deeper than the ancient moss of Blarney,
his claws extended were the coulter
of the gods and a raw March wind
was in his merely agricultural yawn.
Between his back legs was a catapult
of fecundity and he was riggish
as a red-haired man. The girls
of our nation felt him brush their legs
when they were bored with telling rosaries –
at night he clawed their brains in their
coffined beds and his walnut mind
wrinkled on their scalps. His holidays
were upside down in water and then
his face was like the sun: his smell
was in the peat smoke and even his midden
was a harmony of honey. When he stalked
his momentary mice the land shook
as though Atlantic waves were howling
at the western walls. But his eyes
were the greatest thing about him.
They burned low and red so that drunks
saw them like two stars above a hedge,
they held the look of last eyes
in a drowning man, they were the sight
the rebel angels saw the first morning
of expulsion. And he is dead – a voice
from the centre of the earth told of his death

by treachery, that he lies in a hole
of infamy, his kidneys and his liver
torn from his body.

                Therefore tell
the men and horses of the market-place,
the swallows laying twigs, the salmon
on the ladder that nothing is
as it has been
                    time is explored
and all is known, the portents
are of brief and brutal things, since
all must hear the words of desolation,
The King of the Cats is Dead
and it
is only Monday in the world.

Rae Sexton

AT THE CENTRE

At the centre there is a still core.
We will always be kids sitting in the hayfield
in a private world, the tall

grasses feathery with flower, bending
over us, through which we glimpsed
a blue sky unending

where the hovering larks would soar
until they were almost as small
as sandflies and would pour

out their high notes almost beyond reach
of even young ears. The warm straw
and soil lulled us, until we each

found we had nothing more to say
complete in our friendship
feeling this was eternal, this day.

Ralph Bleechmore

NUNS IN PANAMA CITY
Poor Little Sisters

White nuns footless ghostly glide
Spotless cross the city-square
Straight of back and eyes to front
Sweeping past like punctuation
Correct in their articulation
Pressed by neither will nor want
Shapeless blessed by force of habit
They disappear, in evening air.

Ray R Tyndale

ON THE GLENELG TRAM

Forty-eight leather straps
Dance a tango overhead.
Wheels squeal in syncopation.

Sash windows clatter down
Body smells waft past mingled
With flowering wattle.

The conductor orchestrates exits
And entrances, conversing
in Italian.

He must have his regulars,
Know the intimate routines,
The destination of so many;

Know the tourists from the bums
The cheats from the timid
The official from the passing trade.

A man puzzles over his cryptic.
A woman checks her hair in reflection.
A child steams up the window.

All the way we are entranced,
Mesmerised, quite unable to look away
From the young pair entangled before us.

Not coming up for air, oblivious to stares,
Boy's lips grind on girl's orthodontics
For a trip-long kiss.

Ray Stuart

PIONEER CEMETERY
Chain of Ponds, July 1993

The wind
chases clouds
and pushes trash
against the tribute
to Charles Caust

which has been graffiti'd
by an artist unimpressed
with Charles' death at sea in 1906
and the irony that his town
was later drowned as well.

An unweeded path
stops for some reason
halfway up the hill:
like the life of little Percy Hawke
(ceased 1914 – in his eleventh week).

Crosses have been toppled
and headstones smashed,
but Thomasin Symonds
—1861, 53 years—
stands defiant and erect.

Amelia and John are at rest
beneath an oak,
where at least a single carmine flower
appears to have had the common decency
to blossom at their feet.

Richard Tipping

HILLSIDE WITH TWO FIGURES

Mornings without which
sleep. Wet lashes of grass,
black-eyed daisies
folded like old beach umbrellas
in an abandoned paddock, falling away
through unsharpened fences, the fireplace
and the sheep-run
a monument to unnoticed effort.
The apples are crimped
and fallen, all coddle-moth & quince.
Pale buttocks of folding
hillslope and gorge a white bird swoops up
in a pendulum
whoop of song
the licked-clean slope,
tiny fluorescence of flowers
stark thistle and thorn –
the goldtops still asleep
in their deep and foggy roots
there are worlds within the world – creek moss
floating islands
a struggling ant would sink
birds smaller than butterflies
invisible humming wings
that carry us up to a hillside
where you hold me
like a tree hugging rock

Rob Johnson

SQUANDERING

There is no accounting
for the economy of the sea –
its shredding of weed
its cancelled coinage of shell
flung wide on the beach
or pounded into shoals of grit.
The sea is an ageless squanderer
who wastes and wants not –
waste being perhaps the keynote of creation.
Witness the Egyptian Creator God
who took himself in hand and spilt his seed
into the void, begetting earth and sky
and all that followed – the original archetypal
Big Spender. But the texts make clear
the God did it only for pleasure –
creation was incidental. The Indian God
plays with himself at hide and seek
through an infinite multiplicity of forms –
there's really nothing but God
hiding from himself. The Christian God
is more austere – he multiplies himself
only by three. But on any version
creation is only a matter of God
squandering himself in solitude

like the sea beside which I walk
squandering time and thought
watching a girl's long hair
swing as she plays with three ecstatic dogs
who by law ought to be leashed
my skull a sound-shell for the beat
that swells out there and here
thins to a whisper. I squander like the sea
but the wave whispers What matter? What matter?

Robert Clark

THE THRYPTOMENE'S
WHITE CLOUD OF PINK

The thryptomene's white cloud of pink
is flower by tiny flower. Minute
fine threads of rain transmute the hills
to waterfalls of shifting veils
diminishing from crow to dove
in soft perspectives.

My time is spent in small attempts.

Rory Harris

LIGHT

chessboard
winter lawn

dragging my cuffs
through the puddles

chook feeding
by torchlight

bumping my head
on the moon

Shen

FROM ANCESTRAL SHADOWS

I'm so tired
of writing about
being Chinese
as if it were
a loss. I'm a bridge
of compact
words lining a page
brick to brick, a wall
built on a white sheet
of paper –
the colour of mourning.
I'm the professional
weeper at the end
of the funeral, crafting tears
for families too numb
to cry. I'm a street sweeper
flicking litter into
stormwater drains smelling
of shit. I'm the child
that falls because he's too young
to walk. I'm the light suffusing
painted mountains
on paper rolls, edged out of
view as if painting the sun
would have polished the colour
from Chinese art. I'm prosperity
and luck in translation, limited only
by a foreign vocabulary. I'm fire
for ancestral ghosts
who walk in my shade.

And all this
is the past –
the hollow loss
at the center of a lie,
this middle kingdom –
a fist that spreads
pink and red
fingers at dusk
over the sky
as the sun
sets in the east.

Stephanie Tanner

CHARLESTON SCRUB: LATE WINTER

We climb through the fence from the road
into bush that hangs and drips in airy cathedral silence.
Every tree is thin as string, pulled white toward the sky;
leaves spiral slowly down.
Treecreepers and honeyeaters pinpoint the vault
with calls loosely distinct
from their quick bodies.
Water-pods cling to the backs of leaves, then lurch
quickly into space.
A blue gum, its trunk thick as a white pencil blots
the earth with a pile of wet shavings, slippery and black
as writhing eels.
Everywhere you look the banksia men with lidded eyes
like little mouths wink from their perches
and throw a net around you.
Fallen trees slant diagonally over others, like tripped-up
bodies tilted into the after-silence
of the undergrowth,
their hairy roots exposed, fusing the air and clotted like
soft fists of clay.
Rain mists in and smokes us in a white screen; fungi
protrude like lips from the bark and
all that is clear is a small circle of grass
like wet hay beneath our feet.

Stephen Lawrence

HOW NOT TO KILL GOVERNMENT LEADERS

Whenever I'm with the Prime Minister
I want to assassinate him.
Not just pat his shiny head for the media,
say 'Stuffed up. Bad job' – but pull a gun
Bang-Bang. Bang.

We all do. A tic, a scrotal itch implanted
by childhood news reports:
Our generation has lived all its life
with this footage. Foggy blasts of chaos
roost in our minds.

I pat my empty jacket; we stand inside
a magic circle of minders.
Although they know me by now,
they sense the compulsion I endure
and are confused.

Squeezed by a warm scrum of agents,
my trigger-finger snapped,
yanked numb – validating my syndrome,
and their existence, with dim, binding
pressure, steel restraint.

But then he flatters me: 'Admirable launch.'
My neurosis detumesces.
Meaningless CEO flirtation swamps
pricking symptoms, killer brain cells,
with its special drug.

He weakly wrings my weaponless hand.
Eyes drift to the next morsel.
The bright circle browses to another constituent.
I scratch myself. The Prime Minister is safe.
Bastard.

Steve Evans

THE OBSERVER'S GUIDE TO ANGELS
'angels without portfolio' Miroslav Holub

it's the little things you notice
they wear ordinary clothes
but hum next year's hit song
sometimes forget about gravity
stepping too lightly off the kerb
they may have difficulty with
the concept of money
giving the shopkeeper change
and speak a language you've
never heard but somehow understand
angels can't drive
or remember jokes
they have trouble with shoelaces
and instructions on the back of packets
they may compliment you
on your shoulder blades

some gone feral are sleeping rough
and hang out on street corners
talking tough
helpless as dumped kittens
they kiss like Brigitte Bardot
and follow you home
but you can't keep them
not even the fallen ones

Tess Driver

BRIDE WITH A BROOM

Dressed in jeans
she sweeps the floor
around the rigid models dressed in white
plastic virgins stiff in wedding gowns
pure as lacy fantasies, rippling
tucks and folds and curves
hint at promises.

Neat and taut in denim
long hair braided like hope
she sweeps the fearful dust
of betrayal and debt
hard beneath the satin swirls.

Tom Shapcott

THE ELEGY FIRES

The old woman does not tell the nurse
but she has had to reach out
to touch the flames upon her wardrobe.
The wood is uncharred. Around the bed, too,
flames. And last night a hand
beside her own. Eyesight failing,
and the ghost fires, she stared again
to make sure – the hand of her own mother.

With her own unfamiliar hands, lost
for words, she begins the letter
to her son and the date she writes
is ten years out. Ten years, burnt out
as if they had never mottled her
and no ash. Ten years,
ten leaves out of a diary
and her palms are the colour of old newsprint.
'Why do you never write?' One page,
one line of script, ten years, forty years.

Abridgements, she made her virtue out of discarding things.
The bookcase to one daughter, the Doulton to another.
She rid herself of a lifetime's possessions. Her children
have weathered squinting faces, ash-grey hair.
In the unconsuming fire what may return in a vortex? Two children
splashing, green woollen bathers hugging into the creases.
Even the sudden gust of shoreline seaweed that made her hurry them on
to somewhere cleaner, how could that come back? Each grain
in her ocean-damp sandshoes bound again, knotted tight,
as if she still had young feet.

Where is the nurse? She has let go everything
but the ring on her strong, useless, mottled hand.
The bitter arguments of those middle years have been let go,
the long sea-trip back home with little Grace
when she had to discover finally there was nothing left
in Andover. The fretting over money. Parched summers
year after year. Not all things return.
The flames caress her hands
they hover round her body as if she had no body.
This is not her body, this parody crumpled under sheets.
Flames without heat. Years of purpose drawn up,
hours of waiting.
Hours of work in kitchens, committees,
minutes alone with dew speaking down by the fowl-run, minutes.

She stares for focus, she will outstare flames.
Focus is difficult now, rainbow. She is betrayed
as once in childhood she was mocked
by a fractured spectrum.

Is this memory? Out loud her voice is a phone-call,
close but cupped in. 'What parts of our brain function
to achieve this? I know the flames are hallucination.'
No, she will not disturb the nurses.
The flames are visible. The hand of her mother
is visible. She knows, soon, there will be the voices.

Fifty years since her mother whispered. Things that come back
to choose her are not of her deciding. Must she now
endure everything?
Her son, who came this morning, has not returned
for ten years, forty years. That person is not her daughter.
Updraught. If only her mother's hand were comforting:
it is another claimant. If you do not give
it shall be taken. What you give away
shall return a thousandfold.

Yve Louis

OYSTERS

(I do not speak of)
tender oysters
taken from the shell
on tiny forks

the sea's reaped
chill
against the lips

(I do not mention)
bits of grit
silted
between the teeth

or
lemon-tanged
satin
will slip
along the tongue

      (I ask only)
          hold . . .
just on the tip

FRIENDLY STREET PUBLICATIONS

In the first thirty years since its inception, Friendly Street published more than 70 books. These comprised:

- 30 annual anthologies since 1977, representing the best of the year's Friendly Street public readings, plus two other anthologies;
- 11 volumes in the New Poets series, which, since 1995, have each introduced three new writers; and
- 29 individual or shared poetry collections, published in even years (and launched at Writers' Week in the Adelaide Festival of Arts) since 1982.

This activity, initially undertaken with the Adelaide University Union Press but mostly in association with Wakefield Press, has started the publishing careers of many poets who have gone on to national recognition.

The lists shown below are presented in order of publication. More details of the books and information on the authors are available at the Friendly Street web site (http://www.friendlystreetpoets.org.au), and a number of the titles are still available from Wakefield Press at PO Box 2266, Kent Town, South Australia 5071, Australia (http://www.wakefieldpress.com.au).

FRIENDLY STREET READERS

The Friendly Street Poetry Reader, editor Richard Tipping (1977)

No 2 Friendly Street Poetry Reader, editors Ian Reid & Andrew Taylor (1978)

No 3 Friendly Street Poetry Reader, editors Larry Buttrose & Peter Goldsworthy (1979)

No 4 Friendly Street Poetry Reader, editors Span & Jenny Boult (1980)

No 5 Friendly Street Poetry Reader, editors Nancy Gordon & K.F. Pearson (1981)

No 6 Friendly Street Poetry Reader, editors Anne Brewster & Rob Johnson (1982)

No 7 Friendly Street Poetry Reader, editors John Bray & Jan Owen (1983)

No 8 Friendly Street Poetry Reader, editors Robert Clark & Jeri Kroll (1984)

No 9 Friendly Street Poetry Reader, editors Graham Rowlands & Pauline Wardleworth (1985)

No 10 Friendly Street Poetry Reader, editors Rory Harris & Beate Josephi (1986)

No 11 Friendly Street Poetry Reader, editors Elaine Golding & Peter McFarlane (1987)

No 12 Friendly Street Poetry Reader, editors Jeff Guess & Donna McSkimming (1988)

No 13 Friendly Street Poetry Reader, editors Constance Frazer & Barry Westburg (1989)

No 14 Friendly Street Poetry Reader, editors Neil Paech & Ann Timoney Jenkin (1990)

No 15 Friendly Street Poetry Reader, editors Adéle Kipping & Mick Bocchino (1991)

No 16 Friendly Street Poetry Reader, editors Peter McFarlane & Elizabeth Mansutti (1992)

No 17 Friendly Street Poetry Reader, editors Caroline Cleland & John Griffin (1993)

No 18 Friendly Street Poetry Reader, editors Yve Louis & Jeff Guess (1994)

No 19 Friendly Street Poetry Reader, editors Peter Eason & Anna Brooks (1995)

No 20 Friendly Street Poetry Reader, editors Judy Dally & Geoff Kemp (1996)

No 21 Friendly Street Poetry Reader, editors Rae Sexton & Glen Murdoch (1997)

No 22 Friendly Street Poetry Reader, editors Susan McGowan & David Cookson (1998)

Beating Time in a Gothic Space: No 23 Friendly Street Poetry Reader, editors Deb Matthews & Stephen Lawrence (1999)

No 24 Friendly Street Poetry Reader, editors Jude Aquilina & Ray Stuart (2000)

Flow: No 25 Friendly Street Poetry Reader, editors Richard Hillman & Heather Sladdin (2001)

Friendly Street Poetry Reader 26, editors Ioana Petrescu & David Adès (2002)

Blue: Friendly Street 27, editors K*m Mann & Graham Catt (2003)

Another Universe: Friendly Street Poets 28, editors Kate Deller-Evans & Steve Evans (2004)

Blur: Friendly Street Poets 29, editors Shen & Amelia Walker (2005)

Friendly Street Poets Thirty, editors rob walker & Louise Nicholas (2006)

Unruly Sun: Friendly Street Poets 31, editors Erica Jolly & Ivan G. Rehorek (2007)

OTHER ANTHOLOGIES

The Inner Courtyard: A South Australian Anthology of Love Poetry,
     editors Anne Brewster & Jeff Guess (1990)
Tuesday Night Live: Fifteen Years of Friendly Street, editors Jeri Kroll &
     Barry Westburg (1993)

INDIVIDUAL AND COMBINED COLLECTIONS

The Leichardt Heater Journey, Larry Buttrose (1982)
Trader Kate and The Elephants, Kate Llewellyn (1982)
Dial-A-Poem, Graham Rowlands (1982)
Death as Mr Right, Jeri Kroll (1982)
over the outrow, Rory Harris (1982)
The Crack in the Crib, Mike Ladd (1984)
Messages of Things, K.F. Pearson (1984)
the white rose & the bath, Jenny Boult (1984)
Caught on the Hop, Rob Johnson (1984)
Leaving Maps, Jeff Guess (1984)
The Bay of Salamis and Other Poems, John Bray (1986)
No Collars No Cuffs, Geoff Goodfellow (1986)
Beware the Bougainvillea, Donna McSkimming (1986)
the bitumen rhino, neil paech (1986)
in the half-light, Louise Crisp & Valery Wilde (1988)
Other Ways of Looking, Constance Frazer (1988)
snapshots from a moving train, Rory Harris (1988)
On the Menu, Graham Rowlands (1988)
The Fernhouse Cure, Barry Westburg (1988)
Edison Doesn't Invent the Car, Steve Evans (1990)
three's company, Deborah McCulloch, Donna McSkimming &
     Elizabeth Biff Ward (1992)
Across the Gulf, Miriel Lenore, Adele Kipping & Judy Dally (1992)
Picture's Edge, Mike Ladd (1994)
Skinning Time, Graeme Webster (1996)
Beasts Labial, Stephen Lawrence (1998)

Knifing the Ice, Jude Aquilina (2000)
Each Goldfish is Handpainted, Jules Leigh Koch (2002)
Leaving the Mickey, Patricia Irvine (2004)
Women With Their Faces On Fire, Annette Marner (2006)

FRIENDLY STREET NEW POETS SERIES

Friendly Street New Poets 1: *The wolf stares in*, Geoff Kemp; *Silver from Black*,
Yve Louis; *Suburban Bonsai*, John Malone (1995)

Friendly Street New Poets 2: *Picking up the Pieces*, Anna Brooks; *Life in the
Oort Cloud*, Jenny Weight; *Scarves of Sand*, David Cookson (1996)

Friendly Street New Poets 3: *The Red Shoes*, Louise Nicholas; *Her Mother's Arms*,
Stephen Lawrence; *Mending the Dingo Fence*, Richard Hillman (1997)

Friendly Street New Poets 4: *The Right Side of My Face*, Junice Direen;
A Strip of Negatives, Jules Leigh Koch; *Boy Stunner*, Jason Sweeney (1998)

Friendly Street New Poets 5: *I Say . . .* Ioana Petrescu; *Twisting the Rainbow*,
Maureen Vale; *The Love Within My Stare*, Julian A. Zytnik (1999)

Friendly Street New Poets 6: *Rain Falls on the Garden*, John De Laine;
Fish Star Glinting, Alison Manthorpe; *maiden voyage*, Ray R. Tyndale (2000)

Friendly Street New Poets 7: *Travelling with Bligh*, Kate Deller-Evans;
Night Fishing, Jim Puckridge; *Triangular Light*, Melanie Duckworth (2002)

Friendly Street New Poets 8: *The Windmill's Song*, Elaine Barker; *Kite Lady*,
Tess Driver; *Fine Rain Straight Down*, David Mortimer (2003)

Friendly Street New Poets 9: *Peeling Onions*, Jill Gloyne; *Crescent Moon
Caught Me*, Judith Ahmed; *Scoffing Gnocchi*, Linda Uphill (2004)

Friendly Street New Poets 10: *Stealing*, Libby Angel; *Deaf Elegies (from Virginia
Woolf's Record Store)*, Robert J. Bloomfield; *Sparrow in an Airport*, rob walker
(2005)

Friendly Street New Poets 11: *low background noise*, Cameron Fuller; *words free*,
Simone G. Matthews; *jars of artefacts*, Rachel Manning (2006)

INDEX

Find out more about Friendly Street books,
poets and events on the website
www.friendlystreetpoets.org.au